THRONES, NATIONAL TRANSFORMATION AND GOOD GOVERNANCE

THRONES, NATIONAL TRANSFORMATION AND GOOD GOVERNANCE

Gbenga Adegbenro

Contents

Dedication

Then I heard every creature in heaven and on earth and under the earth and on the sea, and all that is in them, saying:

"To him who sits on the throne and to the Lamb be praise and honour and glory and power, for ever and ever!" – Revelation 5:13 NIV

Praise be to the name of God for ever and ever; wisdom and power are His. He changes times and seasons; he deposes kings and raises others, he gives wisdom to the wise and knowledge to the discerning." Daniel 2:20, 21 NIV

This book is dedicated to God who sits on the Throne and to the Lamb of God that was slain, yet lives forever and ever. God alone is worthy to receive power, and riches, and wisdom, and strength, and honour, and glory, and blessing for the wisdom to write this book.

Proclamation

May all the kings of the earth praise you, LORD, when they hear what you have decreed: May they sing of the ways of the LORD, for the glory of the LORD is great. Amen

Acknowledgment

I have to start by thanking my awesome wife, Dr. Adebolaji Janet Oluwafadejesukemi Adegbenro for giving me her indescribable support since 1994 and for praying through until this book is published. She is an important part of the principles written in this book.

Writing this book would have been impossible without the roles and sacrifices you have played in establishing the family government. Thank you so much, I am eternally grateful to you my wife of inestimable value.

To the children that God has given unto me, Adesuyi and Toluwanimi Goodness Daramola, Pipeloluwa Mercy Adegbenro and Isuraoluwa Peace Adegbenro, I thank you all for walking in these principles and making it possible for us to establish the Genesis 18:19 mandate.

What makes life better are people who develop and lead others, who share their time to mentor future leaders. Special appreciation to my father and my mother in the faith, Daddy Emeka and Mummy Bade Nwankpa. I learnt what it means to serve God sacrificially from you. May you see the travails of your soul and be satisfied.

Special thanks to Ina Vermaak and Marelize Nolan, for supporting and praying for us since the year 2013 till today. It will take eternity to reveal what you have done in the secret place of prayer to sustain this work progressively.

I must acknowledge Cecilia Kleynhans, a wonderful sister who has been part of the global thrones movement consistently and has become a teacher of the principles elucidated in this book. Cecilia, I am persuaded of greater things concerning you in this generation.

A big thank you to Dr. Yemi E. Ajimatanrareje, the Senior Pastor of Open Heavens Community Church, Brentwood California USA. Part of this book were written and typed in your house in Brentwood when you hosted me for four months from May to August 2023.

A very special thanks to Pastor Wole Oladiyun, the Senior Pastor of CLAM, Lagos, for his encouragement, for he has this to his credit that he will always ask me when is the book going to come out. Thank you P.W.O.

Pastor Moses Babajide and Pastor Mrs Olubukola Helen Idowu, thank you for being a friend indeed that we can trust come rain come sunshine. Always ready and available to assist, may God reward you for all your sacrifices of love.

The same goes to Apostle Jeshurun Chukwu, who for more than twenty years has been a companion in the pursuit of the vision and the purpose of God. May you see and reap the fruits of your labours in Jesus Name. Thank you for your support all these years.

To Dr. Adedapo and Dr. Mrs Adejoke Adeyinka, a wonderful couple who with passion and great love always minister to our needs; may God reward your sacrifices and labours of love with a mighty visitation in the name of Jesus Christ.

I will like to appreciate Frik and Reneé Schoeman, for their support, together with Desiree Schoeman for embracing this global movement which led to the transformation of Ivydale community in the year 2021.

My heartfelt gratitude to Apostle Peter and Reverend (Mrs) Temitope Oluwole, Founder of Christ Salvation and Praises Evangelical Ministry International. I cannot but remember the remarkable visitation I had with God when your ministry hosted me in Indianapolis in June 2023 and August 2023. More so, when I learnt later my coming at that point in time was based on the covenant you and your wife made with God.

To my wonderful editor, Pastor Eberechukwu Adebayo Nwankpa; thank you for indeed you painstakingly edited the manuscript. Your ideas and wonderful contributions have enriched the outcome of this book in no small way. God bless you.

My publisher, Samuel O. Adeyemi; 'The Media DNA' deserves my appreciation since my engagement with him even though I have not met him physically. Your brilliant ideas and suggestions as a media strategist are commendable.

To all the kings (monarchs) and leaders that I have had the opportunity to lead and minister in their communities and domains of influence with the principles contained in this book, I salute your courage for standing for the truth to establish the supremacy of God on your thrones.

Finally, to all the individuals I have had the privilege to lead and mentor in all corners of the world, those who are working directly with us and those who are now on their own throne assignments: I want to say thank you for being a part of the inspiration of this book. You are all appreciated.

Introduction

This book is a product of God's revelation as well as our engagement with kings (monarchs), political leaders, governors and various people in leadership positions. It is a result of what we have seen, what we have heard and what our hands have handled over the years with regard to the business of thrones. The business of thrones is a mystery with unique fundamentals, complex dynamics and uncommon mechanisms that every king, leader and anyone aspiring to or in a position of power and authority must understand in order to sustainably transform their territories and domains of influence.

This book is an attempt to present the throne paradigm that is needed to establish righteous government and good governance from the basic principles written in the Word of God. The book provides concepts and timeless principles that can be adopted by anyone and everyone in order to positively impact their domain of influence in our very complex world, to advance the transformative power of God for themselves, marriages, families, workplaces, kingdoms, domains of influence and nations. Moral failures and character flaws of leaders have continued to cause dire consequences in many nations of the world especially the nations of Africa. With all the leadership development theories and development, the following questions are still begging for answers:

- Why are majority of leaders so corrupt?
- What makes kings and leaders fail in their leadership responsibilities?
- Why do some leaders start well, but later become a major problem if not a curse to their territory or nation?
- Why are some kings and leaders hindered by challenges they cannot even explain when they are on the throne?

Can We Find Such A One As This?
The dearth of righteous leaders is still a problem in many territories,

organisations and nations. Every domain needs someone to establish righteousness and justice, to proffer solutions to the many-sided and complicated issues in the land and the nation. However, the question about righteous government and good governance in every domain is: **'Can we find such a one as this; a man in whom the Spirit of God is?'** This was the case in Egypt when Pharaoh, the king had a dream concerning God's redemptive purpose for the nation, but there was none of his wise men who could interpret them unto Pharaoh until Joseph was brought up. Joseph did not just interpret the king's dream, he established 14 years grain reserve development plan that saved the nation.

The Challenges to Overcome

To appreciate the crucial importance of excellent visionary leaders like Joseph, consider an alternative reality. Imagine for a moment that there was no one to interpret Pharaoh's dream. In this scenario, Pharaoh would not have known what his dreams meant. However, despite his ignorance, the events foretold in the dream would have come to pass. Egypt would have had a bumper seven years, and following it an unrelenting and ruinous seven years of famine that would completely obliterate the gains of the years of plenty. Crucially, there would have been no one to counsel the storage and preservation of grain during the bumper years, with the result that the famine would have destroyed Egypt. The challenge of good leadership has serious real-world consequences

- The challenge we have is how do we raise men and women with capacity to establish righteousness, justice and good governance.
- Where can they be found?
- How do we train men and women and strategically prepare them for their throne assignments?
- What should be the training modules?
- How do we even raise thrones of righteousness in the land and our nations?
- What are the processes to contend with and overthrow wicked thrones in order to establish righteous thrones?

This book is an attempt to address the above inadequacies and to open the eyes of our understanding to see sustainable transformation and good governance from the throne's paradigm and perspective, by modelling priesthood on the thrones. The book also demonstrates the need to intentionally train people with the vision for thrones, and establish short-term and long-term strategic processes for enthroning righteous people who are well-equipped to establish sustainable transformation, righteousness, justice and good governance. The most productive years of your life are hopefully ahead of you. As you read this book, you may discover that all of your life's experiences before this time were actually a preparation toward one goal which is to rule and reign on the earth, establishing righteousness and justice in your private and public engagements.

The time for destiny fulfilment is NOW!

1.

KINGS AND THRONES

Kings and thrones have been important and very critical concepts in human history. They represent the height of power and authority in all domains. Even though these concepts have evolved in modern times, they remain highly relevant both materially and particularly spiritually. Understanding the concepts of kingship and thrones is important in order to establish the ideals that will empower men and women with the knowledge and the right mind-set to fulfil their throne mandate which will enhance sustainable transformation in all domains of influence.

The Concept of a King

Kings are central to the governance of societies and organisations with the responsibilities for protecting their territories, maintaining social order and providing for the welfare of their people. Kings play a vital role as symbols of unity and cultural identity.

- King – is the ruler, crowned- head and sovereign of a kingdom, a nation and a territory. The king is the decision-maker, a judge and a voice to his people with great responsibility to represent God on the throne.
- A king undertakes a unifying role that is responsible for bringing together various groups or domains that constitute the society.
- In contemporary times, the person may be a king or queen, a president, a governor, a high priest, community head, or a judge with authority to make decisions that affects their domains of influence and nations.

The Concept of a Throne

A throne is a seat occupied by a king which symbolises authority, power, sovereignty, leadership and influence. Thrones have been a central part of human history as a seat or chair reserved for the ruling figure in a hierarchy. Significantly, a throne is a representation of the legitimacy of a ruler, the nobility of kingship, the responsibilities that comes with governance as well as the link to the traditions and history of the kingdom or nation. Historically, the concept of a throne has been tied to a monarchy whereby a single individual has the supreme power to govern a territory or a state. However, the concept of a throne has expanded beyond monarchies. Figuratively, a throne can be used to describe positions of power, authority, or influence in various fields, such as the family, religion, business, workplaces, politics and government of nations.

- A throne is a royal seat of power—the highest place of authority in any given realm. It's a place from which a ruler reigns, acts on behalf of His people, to establish righteousness and justice.
- A throne is not only about the king or the leader. It comprises of other key players that influence the king like the queen, the princes, chiefs or nobles (administrators), courtiers, and many other figures and stakeholders around the throne.
- The throne is the framework of government and governance. It influences the one on the throne, the people, territory, the economy and political life of a nation.

The Kingship Mandate

From the creation mandate in Genesis Chapter One, we received a kingship mandate – to have dominion and develop institutions upon the earth. Made in the image of God, crowned with glory and honour; empowered with dignity and potentials of a king, we are called to faithfully manifest that image in our day-to-day work under God's authority. This mandate is the kingship mandate and it is the starting point for all human government. We govern because he governs and throughout all ages God keeps calling people back to this task of governing.

The Kingship of All Believers

God's original plan in creating man is to have a kingdom of priests established to reign on the earth which is fulfilled through priesthood and kingship. The priesthood empowers mankind to have the image of God, and the kingship empowers mankind to have dominion and authority of God over creations. The redemption in Jesus Christ is not limited to any one area of the creation, not only persons, but nations, kingdoms, the entire creation is to be administered.

- Kingship of All Believers: God is the universal King over all His creation and through redemption, He has bestowed kingship to all believers – Genesis 1:26; Psalm 8; Luke 1:32; Rev. 1:5,6; Rev. 5:9,10
- God destined all believers to occupy two positions – Kingship and Priesthood.
- The kingship is for the Lord's authority and dominion to rule and to reign on the earth as His ambassadors on the thrones.
- The Priesthood is for God's expression to minster to God and to offer sacrifices on behalf of others so that His kingdom will be established on earth.
- All believers can bring transformation to society once they understand the full meaning and practical applications of this redemptive mandate and power
- In this redemptive power and purpose, all believers are kings with throne assignments to rule and to reign on the earth.
- Unfortunately, not all believers have truly and genuinely regained their kingship identity, crown, glory and honour.
- Identity crisis is the bane of the society. It is the root of loss of greatness, bad and corrupt leadership.

The Operational Description of Thrones

The operational description of thrones is the position of kings, rulers, government, leaders (religious, corporate and political), parents, guardians and educators, whereby those who occupy thrones have the privilege and responsibility to nurture, steer, guide, supervise, direct, lead, oversee and assert authority over others, be it a household, small groups, organisation, kingdom, community, territory and the nation – this is a very crucial aspect of developing the right throne mentality.

The prosperity or otherwise of any people, organisation, community, tribe and nation is to some extent dependent on the proper and judicious use of these positions of authority or influence. One of the best examples of the proper stewardship of a family throne is found in (Genesis 18:19). ***"For I know him, that he will command his children and his household after him, and they shall keep the way of the LORD, to do justice and judgment; that the LORD may bring upon Abraham that which he hath spoken of him."***

God's commendation of Father Abraham is a clear example of the establishment of the Family Throne, because the purpose of a throne is to establish righteousness and justice. The family must be seen as the beginning of God's government on the earth. Fatherhood makes a difference in families and by extension the society. A nation is as strong as the families that make up the nation. God expects us to build strong nations by building strong families like Abraham did to build a home where God sits on the throne of every heart establishing righteousness and justice. Your throne therefore is primarily your domain where you exercise influence in order to establish righteousness and justice that God's purpose of peace, prosperity, transformation and development may be implemented and not compromised.

The Thrones Paradigm

The thrones paradigm is essentially a way of thinking, a mindset. A person with this mindset understands that we are all responsible for one throne or another. We are therefore stewards with a responsibility to secure, promote and develop the thrones we occupy. To do this, we must see the transformation from the patterns, lenses, and perspectives of the power of thrones and the spiritual energies of kings and all people in authority.

It is also the paradigm shift of securing the future by raising royal personalities today for future deliverance tomorrow like Mordecai, the Jew did for Esther in the Bible. They were two people who used a deep knowledge of the power of thrones to shape the history of their nation for good. Looking back with the benefit of hindsight, it is clear that Mordecai trained and mentored Esther for successful throne dynamics and ultimate victory. Mordecai himself excelled in his interaction with the throne and attained a position of high elevation, greatness and influence through his knowledge and development of the throne paradigm.

The throne is a place of strategy, power, authority, and influence; and the main purpose of the throne is to establish righteousness and to carry out justice. However, for people to be effective and successful on their mandate and assignment on the thrones, they must be properly trained, their hearts must be well prepared to establish the purpose of the thrones without compromise. The thrones paradigm must be taught and embraced as a veritable tool and resource for the transformation of communities and nations. This throne paradigm must be taught as the operating principles of thrones with emphasis on the integrity of heart and skillfulness of hands as the basic ingredient for national transformation and sustainable development. It is written concerning King David that he led the nation of Israel with integrity of heart, uprightness and skilfulness of hands (Psalm 78:72).

We must understand that socio-economic progress, public order, good governance and prosperity do not follow the natural order of things, we need serious commitment, strong determination and concerted efforts to face the brutal facts of the past and reshape history by laying a proper foundation for the future of our communities and nations. We must engage with this throne paradigm with due diligence and uncommon audacity, blueprints, actionable plans and implementation of both short-term and long-term strategies to unseat the thrones of wickedness in the land and open the gates for the righteous thrones and nations that establish truth.

Key Features of the Throne Paradigm and Operating on the Thrones

- Restoring and developing kingly mentality, throne mentality and values
- Restoring stewardship of family values, thrones and governance.
- The restoration of the priesthood, kingship and the mandate for the thrones.
- Redeeming the thrones and dealing with the foundations of thrones that hinder people on the thrones from doing the right things, the foundations that promote bad leadership and redeeming the land using the influence and power of kings and thrones.
- Establishing justice and righteousness – making things right and doing right, establishing social justice in all domains of influence.
- Dealing with the spirits which destroy leaders (kings and royal

seeds), removal of wickedness from the thrones of the land, raising, establishing and mentoring the righteous on the thrones in every place.
- Leading with integrity of heart, skilfulness of hands, competence, excellent spirit, dealing with the culture of greed, laziness and corruption, establishing righteousness, administering justice and ruling in the fear of God.
- Establish the fear and the worship of God on the throne, institutionalize pragmatic socio-spiritual and socio-economic interventions and providing solutions to the problems of society.

Conclusion

Having this understanding, it is pertinent to emphasize that the empowerment programs and mentorship for throne assignment must be conceptualized and intentionally programmed into the fabric of life from birth, in our families, educational institutions and every structure in the society in order to establish good governance and sustainable development among the nations.

2.

THE THRONE OF GOD

God's Throne Revealed – (Revelations 4 & 5)

There is a throne in heaven, and the LORD God sits upon it as the sovereign ruler of the universe! This is the central fact of heaven; that there is *an occupied throne* in heaven. ***"..Behold, a throne was set in heaven, and one sat on the throne..."*** (Revelation 4:2). The throne and the one who sits on the throne was the centrepiece of John's vision of heaven in the Book of revelation and everything else is described with reverence to this throne.

With this heavenly perspective in connection with what happens on the earth, it is certain that mankind cannot do without the concept of a throne, a ruler. The throne activities depicted in Revelation chapters four and five gives us a vivid and profound picture about the throne of God as the literal and figurative symbol of His all-consuming glory and infinite sovereignty. The throne is a powerful declaration of not merely God's presence, but of His sovereign, rightful reign, and His prerogative to judge.

We have to settle it in our mind that there is an occupied throne in heaven, and the God of the Bible rules from the throne. The throne of God is described as a majestic throne surrounded by a rainbow, with twenty-four elders, living creatures, myriads of angels, the seven spirits before the throne and the Lamb, but in all everyone need a personal encounter in the revelation of His Throne because it is beyond what anyone can describe for you or write about – it is indeed a mystery. God is upon His Throne in heaven ruling the affairs of men on earth. Unlike earthly monarchs who are bound by time and territory, God's throne represents His transcendent reign over the whole universe for all eternity.

We need to understand the concepts of kings and thrones from God's perspective in order to harness the full benefits of the purpose of thrones because He is the King of kings and all thrones belong to Him, even though many kings and thrones are working in rebellion to His Throne (Psalm 2). Again, Revelation Chapter Five depicts the worthiness of the Lamb, the victory of the Lamb, the redemption He accomplished, the purpose of the redemption and the immediate worship that followed by all creation both in heaven and on the earth. As a result of the redemption accomplished, we have been made kings and priests to reign on the earth.

> *"You are worthy to take the scroll, And to open its seals; For You were slain, And have redeemed us to God by Your blood Out of every tribe and tongue and people and nation, And have made us kings and priests to our God; And we shall reign on the earth."* Revelation 5:9, **10.**

We must settle the fact that all believers are kings and priests, redeemed by the sacrifice of the Lamb and ordained by God to rule and to reign on the earth to establish dominion, develop institutions, and establish government in righteousness and justice as His kings on the earth. This we can only accomplish effectively and efficiently when we see the revelation of thrones, understand God's perspective of thrones and truly regain our kingly identity.

Characteristics and Manifestations of God's Throne

By the record of John in Revelation Chapters Four and Five, we could see the awe-inspiring spiritual realities surrounding God and His throne. John, speaking in symbolic language, provided a dynamic description of God's throne and the activities surrounding it. The descriptions of John and other Bible references provided us with the characteristics and the manifestations of God's Throne.

- ### Throne of Glorious Majesty

The prophetic vision began with a clear focus on the throne of God, and this throne refers not only to the throne but to the entire throne room. In the opening stage of this vision, John focuses on the majestic glory of God. John saw a throne set in heaven which he described around four prepositional phrases: on the throne; round about the throne; out of the throne; and before the throne. God's throne is an epitome of majesty – impressive dignity and beauty that is indescribable. The takeaway here is that every king and leader must marvel at the glorious majesty of God, the King of kings and the LORD of Lords. To do otherwise will be a rebellion against God.

· **Throne of Sovereignty**

When the Bible speaks of God's throne, the real emphasis is on God's sovereign rule and transcendence – He is the God of the whole universe. We see from John's description that Heaven has many moving parts – The Lamb, the four beasts, the twenty-four elders, and an innumerable company of angelic beings. However, all these are referred to as one entity – God's Throne. This means that everyone and everything in heaven revolves around God's Throne. This understanding gives us an idea of how far reaching and all-encompassing God's Throne is. Psalm 103:19 says ***"The LORD has established His throne in heaven, and His kingdom rules over all."*** No throne rooms on earth, executive offices, legislative halls, or courtrooms come anywhere close to rivalling the authority and sovereignty of God's throne. The takeaway here is that kings and leaders must be instructed in what the Psalmist declared in Psalms: "***Now therefore, be wise, O kings; be instructed, you judges of the earth. Serve the Lord with fear and rejoice with trembling. Kiss the Son, lest he be angry, and you perish in the way, when his wrath is kindled but a little. Blessed are all those who put their trust in him***" (Psalms 2:10-12). As we marvel at the majesty of God, we should bow like the elders before the sovereignty of God.

· **Throne established on a perfect sacrifice and covenant**

The throne of God is established on the perfect sacrifice of the Lamb of God and a covenant. Most of the earthly thrones are established on the sacrifices of animals and covenant to the gods of the land. The implication of this is that anyone in a position of authority has the responsibility to break every occultic and satanic covenant on the throne and bring their thrones into covenant with the Throne of God through the blood of the everlasting covenant.

· **Throne surrounded by a Rainbow**

God's throne is surrounded by a rainbow. The rainbow is a reminder of God's commitment to His covenant with man that He will not destroy the earth with water (Genesis 9:11-17). God has a reminder of His promise to never destroy the earth again with water, a promise that directs His sovereignty. Thus, the rainbow symbolizes God's mercy and grace in the midst of divine judgment. The throne of God is established for the preservation of life. In heaven, John sees "***the river of the water of life, as clear as crystal, flowing from the throne of God and of the Lamb***" – Revelation 22:1.

· **Throne Established with Council of Twenty-Four Elders**

Surrounding the throne of God are 22 other lesser thrones and seated upon these thrones are 24 elders as written in Revelation 4:4. We don't know precisely who these 24 elders are, but the fact that they sit upon thrones with golden crowns on their heads indicates that they reign with Him. And the fact that they are called elders indicate that they are matured personality full of wisdom that can be entrusted with governmental affairs. This is very instructive because kings of the earth cannot rule in isolation, they must surround themselves with people with sound wisdom to bear rule with them.

· **The Seven Spirits before His Throne**

In Revelation 4:5, the seven spirits of God are symbolized as seven burning lamps that are before God's throne. In Revelation 5:6 the seven spirits are the "seven eyes" of the Lamb, and they are "sent out into all the earth." These seven spirits are identified in Isaiah 11:1-5 as The Spirit of the Lord, the Spirit of Wisdom and Understanding, the Spirit of Counsel and Might, the Spirit of Knowledge and the Spirit of the Fear of the Lord. Kings and leaders are expected to operate on their thrones by the Seven Spirits of God. We have written a book and manual on the Seven Spirits of God to operate on the thrones available on Amazon.

- **Throne Established for Perfect Justice**

The greatness of God is demonstrated by His righteous judgments and His righteous judgments are executed from His throne: ***"But the LORD shall endure for ever: he hath prepared his throne for judgement. And he shall judge the world in righteousness, he shall minister judgment to the people in uprightness."*** (Psalms 9:7, 8). God's throne manifests perfect justice and he expects earthly thrones to manifest righteousness and justice. The Judgement of King Solomon recorded in 1Kings 3:16-28 is a manifestation of perfect judgment. Two mothers living in the same house, each the mother of an infant son, came to Solomon. One of the babies had died, and each claimed the living boy as her own.

Calling for a sword, Solomon declared his judgment: he ordained the disputed infant be divided into two parts, each woman to receive one part. One mother did not contest the ruling, declaring that if she could not have the baby then neither of them could, but the other begged Solomon, "Give the baby to her, just don't kill him!" The king declared the second woman the true mother, as a mother would even give up her baby if that was necessary to save its life. ***"All Israel heard of the judgment that the king had rendered, and they stood in awe of the king because they perceived the wisdom of God was in him to do justice."*** (1 Kings 3:28). The judgment of Solomon takes the king to even loftier heights, inspiring national reference for their leader and established the influence of his throne beyond Israel, many leaders will later travel to Israel to seek the wisdom of God.

- **Throne Established on Four Pillars**

The throne of God is built on four pillars or foundations:

Righteousness – The attribute of God as the law giver and one that has power to input His righteousness to mankind through faith in

Christ Jesus resulting in the ability to do what is right and live according to His righteous demands. A throne that abhors wickedness. Wrong living threatens human lives everywhere.

Justice – God is just. It is His character in which He exhibits sound judgement always and through which He sets the standard of justice. A throne of perfect justice.

Mercy – The character and disposition to show compassion, kindness, forgiveness and leniency to the guilty or offender. The desire to show mercy –Hosea 6:6.

Truth – *Truth is that which is consistent with the mind, will, character, glory, and being of God.* It is that which is also in agreement with reality which manifests in sincerity in character, action and utterance.

God expect the earthly thrones to be established and operated on these pillars and foundations of Righteousness, Justice, Mercy and Truth.

· **Throne Established for Worship**

Everything about the throne of God is centred on the worship of Him who lives forever. The living creatures constantly worship God, the 24 elders worship the enthroned God. A kingdom or territory resembles what they worship. The primary responsibility of every king or leader is to establish the worship of the living God in their domain, as against the worship of other gods that have not made the heavens and the earth. This is sacrosanct.

3.

ALL THRONES BELONG TO GOD

God's Sovereignty and Ownership over Everything

It starts with creation itself and the very fact that God made everything and then put mankind over His creation – Genesis 1 and 2. The most dangerous misconception that can enter the heart of any king or leader is to believe that he/she got to the throne by his/her own power or the idea that the throne or position you occupied belong to you and not God. Many of the problems with many kings and people in leadership position begin when they forget that God is the King and the owner of the whole universe. King David, the most dynamic king of Israel testified:

"Thine, O LORD, is the greatness, and the power, and the glory, and the victory, and the majesty: for all that is in the heaven and in the earth is thine; thine is the kingdom, O LORD, and thou art exalted as head above all. Both riches and honour come from thee, and thou reignest over all; and in thine hand is power and might; and in thine hand it is to make great, and to give strength unto all". 1 Chronicles 29:11, 12.

Nehemiah, the builder and a great leader also declared:

"You alone are the LORD. You created the heavens, the highest heavens with all their host, the earth and all that is on it, the seas and all that is in them. You give life to all things, and the host of heaven worships You". Nehemiah 9:6.

To demonstrate the all-encompassing nature of Christ's creative power Paul wrote in Colossians 1:16 *"For by him were all things created, that are in heaven, and that are in earth, visible and invisible, whether they be thrones, or dominions, or principalities, or powers: all things were created by him, and for him:"*

Solomon Sat on the Throne of God

A direct reference that the earthly thrones belong to God is expressed where it is written that King Solomon sat on the throne of God.

1 Chronicles 29:23

So Solomon sat on the throne of the LORD as king in place of his father David. He prospered, and all Israel obeyed him.

Thrones represent the seat of government and the only one entitled to sit on it is the legal ruler of that government or kingdom. Does this verse mean that Solomon sat on God's throne in heaven? Absolutely not, but it is implied that the earthly throne of the king belongs to God. It is particularly instructive for everyone in position of leadership and government to note and bear this fact in mind. In a Bible study session during a conference of the Fellowship of Christian Traditional Rulers of Nigeria (FECTRON), this word of the Lord came as a revelation, an eye opener and a major landmark that reset the minds, the attitude and subsequent actions of all the kings that came for the conference.

- First, the kings realised that their throne is God's throne and not the throne of their ancestors. Most traditions belief that the throne belong to the ancestors which bring legitimacy to idolatry and ancestral worship and veneration of past kings on the throne. This became a turning point in the lives of the kings and subsequent teaching on the subject of idolatry on the thrones.
- The kings realised that they are to serve as God's earthly lesser kings and to bring their kingdom under the sovereignty of the King of kings. They must understand that the throne actually belongs to God and they are seating on the throne as God's representative.
- Their allegiance must be to the God, the King of kings and they must not hinder or diminish God's sovereignty over their kingdoms or territories.
- As a matter of fact, they are to draw patterns of kingship, wisdom and counsels from God and the patterns of His throne in order for them to succeed on their thrones.
- This revelation delivered the kings from the fear of the traditions of

the land that subject them to worship other lesser gods and opened their eyes to the need to dedicate themselves and their throne in covenant to the Great King who alone made it possible for them to seat on the throne.

- It made the kings to understand and embrace their mission and purpose on the throne: to do the will of God without fear so that they and their kingdom can prosper.

2 Chronicles 9:8

Blessed be the LORD your God, who has delighted in you to set you on His throne to be king for the LORD your God. Because your God loved Israel enough to establish them forever, He has made you king over them to carry out justice and righteousness.

The Declaration of Queen Sheba

2 Chronicles 9:8 was spoken to King Solomon by Queen Sheba. The pagan Queen Sheba was able to recognise and to remind King Solomon that the throne belongs to God and that it is God that placed him to rule for Him to establish justice and righteousness. As a king or a leader, you need to remind yourself daily that it is God who has placed you in that position and it is imperative to bear it in mind that you are on the throne to execute righteousness and justice all the time. Thus, it will bring great blessings to the king or leader and the nation as well.

Establishing God's Throne on The Earth

The central role of mankind here on earth is to establish the throne of God on earth, to be on the throne for God on earth. This is the dominion mandate of Genesis 1:26-28 and Psalm 8 in the Old Testament of the Bible. In the New Testament, it is the rulership mandate of Revelation 5:9, 10; where the redemptive purpose is clearly stated that the redeemed of the Lord have been made unto God as kings and priests to rule and to reign on the earth. The direct implication is that God's people are ordained with the potentials and ability to establish the throne of God everywhere on the earth having been made unto God as kings and priests. It is therefore critical for you to keep your eyes on the intentional redemptive purpose of God for you in your domain of influence. This is the dimension unto which our kingly identity must be practically restored and deployed to establish righteousness and justice on the earth. If you are to govern the works of God's hands, your kingly identity and character must be formed so you are competent to serve effectively as God's kings and rulers on His throne on the earth.

Rebuilding The Tabernacle of David – Isaiah 16:5, Amos 9:11-12, Acts 15:15-16.

The Tabernacle of David is the name given to the tent that King David set up on Mount Zion in Jerusalem to house the Ark of the Covenant. After placing the Ark in the tent, David the king established an order of worship that continued through his reign. Singers and musicians were employed to praise, give thanks and prophesy before the ark of God. Twenty-four hours a day worship was going on Mount Zion. This is a pattern of throne worship that John saw on the Island of Patmos written in Revelation chapters four and five.

Mount Zion became the worship capital of Israel and also the governmental capital at the same time – This is amazing. King David ran the affairs of the kingdom from Mount Zion. He made laws and passed judgment concerning disputes from Mount Zion. Decisions on whether or not to go to war were made from Mount Zion. All things concerning the kingdom were set in motion from Mount Zion. The Tabernacle of David or the throne of David became the standard and pattern of government, what is it for a throne or government to be established. That is why God promised to rebuild and raise up the tabernacle of David, because it is a throne established on true worship and ideal government and governance.

Amos 9:11, 12
In that day will I raise up the tabernacle of David that is fallen, and close up the breaches thereof; and I will raise up his ruins, and I will build it as in the days of old:
That they may possess the remnant of Edom, and of all the heathen, which are called by my name, saith the Lord that doeth this.

This promise of raising the Tabernacle of David implies the restoration of the patterns of true throne worship, relaying foundations and establishment of righteous governance in tandem with God's ideals of governance. The restoration of David's Tabernacle is the restoration of kingdom worship, authority, righteous government and rulership based on the fear of God together with other kingdom principles. When the Tabernacle of David is rebuilt, the presence of God, the characters of God's throne, His divine nature, principles, values, wisdom and worship will be brought into the kingdoms, governance, workplaces, marketplaces and institutions to establish righteousness and justice. Today this restoration and rebuilding of the Tabernacle of David and the ruins is gathering momentum in fulfilment of what is written in the Psalms by King David:

Psalm 138:4, 5
All the kings of the earth shall praise You, O Lord, when they hear the words of Your mouth.
Yes, they shall sing of the ways of the Lord, for great is the glory of the Lord.

On Saturday 11 August 2001, the Fellowship of Christian Traditional Rulers (FECTRON) was established in Warri, Delta State of Nigeria. Several kings and traditional leaders from different parts of Nigeria were in attendance. Blessed was that day when all the kings led by one of the royal fathers were all face down with their royal regalia in worship of the Almighty God. Today, several kings are members of this fellowship. Most of these kings have not just renounced idolatry on their thrones, they are now apostles, pastors and evangelists with many of them having evangelical churches in their palaces. We have carried out throne cleansing in many of their domains and many have entered into a covenant with God over their throne and land with tremendous transformation and development taking place in their kingdoms. Many of them have established worship centres in their palaces. Moreover, in 2013, we had the first gathering of African kings and queens in Pretoria with kings and queens from different parts of Africa in attendance. It was a nine-day training conference organised by Global Thrones Foundation.

4.

STRATEGIC POSITION OF KINGS

God's Preeminent Kingship

God is the ultimate ruler in the affairs of men and the King of kings, and Lord of lords. The heaven is His Throne and the earth He has given to mankind to possess and in it He has positioned kings, leaders, rulers, and government to assert authority over the land and creation and to implement development and good governance. God's preeminent Kingship is established throughout all generations. It is pertinent to state that all others kings (monarchs, rulers and leaders) are subservient to God and they will be judged by Him as well. The king's heart is in the hand of God and He expect every king and leaders of His people to hearken to His voice, to draw wisdom, understanding and counsels from Him, and to serve and obey Him.

In God's view, only one thing made a good king: "he did what was right and pleasing in the sight of the Lord." And only one thing also made an evil king: "he did what was evil in the sight of the Lord." This is still the same metric He uses today for everyone in the position of leadership – to do what is right before God and men. God in His sovereignty can and has moved the hearts and minds of kings to fulfil His purposes, but if a king rejects the Lord; the Lord will also reject him (1 Samuel 15:3). It is expedient for every leader and those in positions of authority and influence to program their mind-set that God is the ultimate King.

God Removes Kings and Sets up Kings

"The LORD maketh poor, and maketh rich: he bringeth low, and lifteth up. He raiseth up the poor out of the dust, and lifteth up the beggar from the dunghill, to set them among princes, and to make them inherit the throne of glory: for the pillars of the earth are the LORD'S, and he hath set the world upon them." (1 Samuel. 2:7, 8).

"And he changeth the times and the seasons: he removeth kings,

and setteth up kings: he giveth wisdom unto the wise, and knowledge to them that know understanding." (Daniel. 2:21)

What happened to King Nebuchadnezzar should teach all in positions of authority a great lesson. He, King Nebuchadnezzar was one of the greatest kings of the ancient world. God chose to make an example of him to prove His sovereignty and preeminent kingship. He was greatly humiliated by God due to his arrogant pride and refusal to acknowledge God's true Sovereignty over him and his kingdom. As the king was walking on the roof of the royal palace of Babylon, his heart was lifted up in pride and said, "...is not this great Babylon that I have built for the house of the kingdom by the might of my power, and for the honour of my majesty?" While the word was in the king's mouth, there fell a voice from heaven, saying,

"O king Nebuchadnezzar, to thee it is spoken; The kingdom is departed from thee and they shall drive thee from men, and thy dwelling shall be with the beasts of the field: they shall make thee to eat grass as oxen, and seven times shall pass over thee, until thou know that the most High ruleth in the kingdom of men, and giveth it to whomsoever he will." Daniel 4:30-32

However, when the duration of the king's humiliation and punishment was complete, his mind-set was re-programmed and he humbly acknowledged the truth that all mankind, leaders, rulers and kings must fully understand:

"And at the end of the days I Nebuchadnezzar lifted up mine eyes unto heaven, and mine understanding returned unto me, and I blessed the most High, and I praised and honoured him that liveth for ever, whose dominion is an everlasting dominion, and his kingdom is from generation to generation: And all the inhabitants of the earth are reputed as nothing: and he doeth according to his will in the army of heaven, and among the inhabitants of the earth: and none can stay his hand, or say unto him, What doest thou?
At the same time my reason returned unto me; and for the glory of my kingdom, mine honour and brightness returned unto me; and my counsellors and my lords sought unto me; and I was established

in my kingdom, and excellent majesty was added unto me. Now I Nebuchadnezzar praise and extol and honour the King of heaven, all whose works are truth, and his ways judgment: and those that walk-in pride he is able to abase." Daniel 4:34-37

The Spiritual Potentials of Kings

We are made in the image of God and given dominion over everything hence the status of a king. Adam was the first king and was set in charge, to dress, beautify, and develop the garden. Christ has redeemed and made us unto God as kings and priest to reign on the earth. Reigning as kings is deploying the spiritual potentials of the image of God in us in our domain of influence. However, due to ignorance as well as other factors identified in this book, many have wasted the kingly potentials, resources, power and the riches of God's inheritance in them as kings and priests. Redemption is about restoration and repositioning with the spiritual potentials of kings to exercise dominion upon the earth.

Righteousness and Justice is of the Kings

Kings and leaders bear a greater responsibility before God to live, lead and govern righteously and wisely, with mercy, truth and in the fear of God.

"Give the king thy judgments, O God, and thy righteousness unto the king's son. He shall judge thy people with righteousness, and thy poor with judgment. The mountains shall bring peace to the people, and the little hills, by righteousness. He shall judge the poor of the people, he shall save the children of the needy, and shall break in pieces the oppressor." Psalm 72:1-4

- Righteousness is doing right and teaching the right ways of doing things especially defending the vulnerable and standing for what is right.
- Justice is making things right, the quality of being fair to all and equitable to all.
- Judgement is the ability to hand down a decision based on sound principle.

The main focus of throne assignment is doing what is right and carrying out justice at all levels of human endeavour. This is a practical and radical way of life to transform a kingdom, a territory or a nation, but this is not easy because it takes courage to do and establish righteousness and administer justice on the thrones.

Discernment is of Kings

Discernment is the ability to distinguish between what is good and evil in order to arrive at the right decisions and to judge well. It is a demonstration of wisdom and insight that goes beyond what is seen or heard. King Solomon understood that a key component of leadership is wise and sound discernment and so the king asked God for understanding heart and discernment to govern his people:

"So give your servant a discerning heart to govern your people and to distinguish between right and wrong. For who is able to govern this great people of yours?" – 1 Kings 3:9-14.

King Solomon was an epitome of discernment and was known for his power of discernment, making many wise decisions and judgements on the throne. Seeking discernment must become the focus of all kings and leaders who desire to walk righteously and establish justice because discernment is a fundamental ingredient for throne assignment to administer justice (1 kings 3:9, 11). To compromise discernment will bring disaster to kings, their thrones and their people leading to chaos, insecurity and instability in the land. This is true for every person in any position of power, influence and authority.

"My Son, preserve sound judgment and discernment, do not let them out of your sight; they will be life for you, an ornament to grace your neck. Then you will go on your way in safety, and your foot will not stumble; when you lie down, you will not be afraid; when you lie down, your sleep will be sweet." (Proverbs 3:21-24).

Power, Authority and Activities of Kings

Where the word of a king is, there is power: and who may say unto him, what doest thou? (Eccl. 8:4). Power and authority are extremely important concepts of thrones, kings and leadership. Power and authority are the mandate to rule and to reign:

- Power is the ability of an individual to influence others and control their behaviour.
- Authority refers to the legal and formal right to give commands and make decisions.

That is why power and authority must not be corrupted and the reason why King David wrote that "he that rule over men must be just, ruling in the fear of God." (2 Sam.23:3). The moment power and authority are misused or corrupted, there will be chaos in the kingdom, organisation, the land or the nation.

The power and authority of a king is a function of the power and influence of his throne. Of Jesus, the King of kings it is written: 'He shall be great, and shall be called the Son of the Highest: and the Lord God shall give unto him the throne of his father David: And he shall reign over the house of Jacob for ever; and of his kingdom there shall be no end. The same Jesus stated: 'All power is given unto me in heaven and in earth.'(Matthew28:18). And in the last chapter of the bible Jesus made the greatest revolutionary statements concerning all believers in him: 'And hast made us unto our God kings and priests: and we shall reign on the earth.'(Revelation. 5:10).

The activities of a king or a leader are to bring blessings and good fortune to his people and domain of influence, to shepherd, to judge, to be a warlord to secure his people, to act as a priest and a seer, a unifying force, to bring healing, reformation, transformation, rebuilding, a voice for the poor and needy and to restore true worship of God of which the prophetic prototype is the rebuilding of the tabernacle of David. The move of God in these last days is to restore the full status and position of kings, rulers, leaders in order to effectively bring transformation to their domains of influence. This is one aspect of what should be the order of the day and become the focus and passion of everyone who desires to see righteousness and justice established in the society.

5.

DYNAMIC POWERS OF KINGS AND THRONES

Generally, power is the ability to impose your will or make others act in the way you want based on your authority. Power and authority are usually used interchangeably, but they are not the same. Power is the ability or capacity to force, coerce, or manipulate someone or something to do as one pleases. Authority is the legal right to use power. Typically, kings have both authority and power. As a king or a person in authority you hold a source of power over others in which you can demand they act a certain way or carry out specific actions even though they may not think you're right or believe in the same things you do. But, they will perform their actions because you hold a source of power which could result in consequences. However, there are other dynamic powers of kings and thrones that can be deployed to bring transformation in any sphere of influence.

1. **Power of Vison**

Vision is a critical part and tool of leadership and kingship. Every successful endeavour requires a vision. The ability to see the big picture, the future through insights and revelation. That is why God gave King David a vision for the throne. He had a vision for his throne and his kingdom. There is a great power released for people to take actions willingly when the king or leader cast a clear vision for the throne, but where there is no clear vision the people will have nothing to run with. Vision releases the power of engagement.

Psalm 89:19-21

Then thou spakest in vision to thy holy one, and saidst, I have laid help upon one that is mighty; I have exalted one chosen out of the people. I have found David my servant; with my holy oil have I anointed him: With whom my hand shall be established: mine arm also shall strengthen him.

- Vision directs the power of focus
- Vision provides direction
- Vision increases power of creativity
- Vision releases the power of purpose
- Vision energises the life of the king
- Vision transforms us into great leaders

Kings and those in authority must be able to effectively communicate the vison of their kingdoms and organisations for it is the blueprint for progress and advancement. Leaders should be able to set and articulate a vision for growth and development that will outlast them. Vision is about direction, the world will follow a man or woman who knows the road, and where he/she is going, who knows what he/she wants to achieve.

2. **Power of Influence**

Leadership is the ability to influence others. Kings and those in authority have the power of influence, the ability to affect the character, behaviour and development of others. It is the ability to influence others to take action be it in a family or in the nation. Influence is the ability to change how someone else behaves or thinks based on relationships, imitation and persuasion instead of control. The influence of a king can grow even beyond his own domain and kingdom even though he does not have authority over other kingdoms. King Solomon was so renowned for his wisdom that other kings from far away kingdoms came to seek wisdom from him.

3. **Power of Covenant**

We must understand the power and importance of covenant with God on the throne, to make a deliberate and conscious effort to enter into a covenant with God and to bring our sphere of influence into a covenant with God.

The above words were spoken by Hezekiah, the king of Judah. Hezekiah was one of the great leaders of God's people. He came to power when the country was in a mess. His father had led the country down a disastrous path by encouraging the country in moral decline. Because of this, rather than the country enjoying God's blessing, they were facing God's wrath and judgment because of their sins. Hezekiah knew why his country faced the problems they did: They had departed from God.

He also knew what the solution was: They needed to return back to God. Hezekiah employed the power of covenant as a king to return the nation back to the path of greatness. Whenever a king or a leader enters into a covenant with God, the whole land, kingdom and nation is brought into a covenant with God. Asa, the king started his reformation by the power of covenant with God (2 Chronicles 15:12-15). Inheriting a challenging or problematic situation need not be terminal. Where one becomes a leader in a territory or organisation where sin is prevalent, you need to take deliberate decisions to take the wrath of God away and one such decision is to make a covenant with God and bring your domain, territory or organisation into a covenant with the Lord.

4. **Power of Words**

Generally, words are powerful whether spoken or written – all words carry potential power. Death and life are in the power of the tongue, and those who love it will eat its fruit (Proverbs 18:21). The words of a wise man's mouth are gracious and win him favour, but the lips of a fool consume him (Ecclesiastes 10:12). More importantly, the words of a king or a leader are powerful:

Ecclesiastes 8:4
**Where the word of a king is, there is power: and who may say
unto him, what doest thou?**

The choices kings or rulers make with their words set the parameters for what will happen to them, their communities or organisations. Their words can build or destroy, that is why kings and leaders must be skilful in the language they speak to their people. Kings and leaders must learn and know how to use the power of the words well and not given to speaking out of turn.

5. Power of Knowledge

It is said that knowledge is power as well as knowledge is light. Because when you gain knowledge you are empowered and enlightened.

Proverbs 25:2, 3
It is the glory of God to conceal a matter, But the glory of kings is to search out a matter. The heaven for height, and the earth for depth, and the heart of kings is unsearchable.

It is the honour and the glory of kings and all in authority to diligently seek out knowledge and truth because they are daily charged with taking important decisions that will affect other people, their kingdom and nation. As the passage above notes, the matters of a king or leader has to deal with is concealed or hidden. Thus, the ability to seek out relevant information and knowledge is critical. A decision made without understanding and knowing all the facts will be disastrous. Kings and leaders must search out facts diligently before taking decisions. The same principle is applicable to government leaders and everyone in position of authority.

6. Power of Worship

There is something that is fundamental about the nature of human beings, the way they function, why they do the things they do, the nature of human life, the things that shape our choices, decisions, actions, relationships. The most basic and essential function of a human being is worship. Everybody, even the most irreligious person, worships. As a human being, worship is first your identity before it's ever your activity. We were created by God and designed to be worshipers. Worship means that there is always something that lays claim to our hearts that motivates us and directs us.

Worship involves ascribing all glory to God in spirit and truth regardless of circumstances regardless of any height you may attain in life. A deep sense of fellowship and intimacy with God, the King of kings from whom all wisdom to rule and reign flows. Worship is a powerful force. David's worship sent the evil spirits tormenting Saul packing (1 Sam. 16:23).

Psalm 29:1, 2
Give unto the Lord, O ye mighty, give unto the Lord glory and strength. Give unto the Lord the glory due unto his name; worship the Lord in the beauty of holiness.

King David is known as an example of a king who was a true and passionate worshipper of God who used the power of worship to establish his throne:

2 Samuel 6:12-15
Now it was told King David, saying, "The Lord has blessed the house of Obed-Edom and all that belongs to him, because of the ark of God." So David went and brought up the ark of God from the house of Obed-Edom to the City of David with gladness.
And so it was, when those bearing the ark of the Lord had gone six paces, that he sacrificed oxen and fatted sheep.
Then David danced before the Lord with all his might; and David was wearing a linen ephod.
So David and all the house of Israel brought up the ark of the Lord with shouting and with the sound of the trumpet.

King David engaged in worshipping God that nothing else in this world matters to him. His wife Michal equated his action to that of worthless fellows because he was wearing only a linen ephod. But King David was unapologetic, rather he declared that he will celebrate before the Lord who lifted him to inherit the throne and be even be more lightly esteemed than before. He knew the power of fully embracing the art of giving all glory to God. A king and leaders with understanding will bring the glory of God over their domains of influence through the power of worship. Revelation Chapters 4 and 5 indicate that worship is the atmosphere of heaven where God has His Throne.

In the year 2001, The Fellowship of Christian Traditional Rulers of Nigeria (FECTRON) was inaugurated at the palace of His Royal Majesty Atuwatse II of blessed memory in Warri, Delta State of Nigeria. Many high profile first class traditional rulers and their queens were in attendance from the North, South, East and West of Nigeria. During the inauguration, one of the royalties led us in worship, all the kings removed their crowns and laid before God in worship. That act of worship is reminiscent of the elders in heaven who cast their crowns down before God in Revelation 4:10. You could feel the awesome power and presence of the Almighty God, the King of kings. It was as if the Heavens were opened and we were supernaturally aligned with the worship going on in Heaven. It was an otherworldly, out-of-body experience in which time, space and matter seemed irrelevant and inconsequential. Nothing on earth can rival the joy and happiness I felt in God's presence that day.

7. Power of Kingly Identity

Identity plays a critical role in life; it is what drives most of our behaviours and results in life. Identity is the truth of who you are, a function of your potentials and purpose. Your identity informs your mind-set and defines who you are and what you do. The kingly identity is unique. People with kingly mentality operate from a mind-set which affects their attitudes and values. When you gain a perspective of your kingly identity, you are unstoppable. That is why, the Lion is the king of the jungle despite the fact it is not the fastest nor the biggest animal in the jungle. An identity and mind-set of maturity and responsibility is integral to successful leadership. It is possible for a king or a leader to be on the throne with enormous responsibility, and yet be a child (Ecclesiastes 10:16, 17). The heavy responsibility of a king or a leader does not fit a person who is childish at heart and in attitude. Many people are in leadership position who are still babies in every sense of the word – undeveloped in their hearts, attitude, values and kingly identity. The Teacher clearly stated:

Woe to you, O land, when your king is a child and when your [incompetent] officials and princes feast in the morning.

A king or a leader of people must be free from habits that weakens his/her kingly identity, free from behaviours and lifestyles that reduces personal competence and compromise on integrity. The kingly identity enables stability and fruitful engagement with the throne mandate, responsibilities, assignments as well as the challenges. Power flows from a strong and well-balanced sense of Identity.

8. Power of Priesthood

Psalm 110, one of the key passages about the priesthood of Jesus and priesthood in general indicates a key spiritual principle. No throne is effective without a strong priesthood. This is why Jesus is the priest of God's throne in heaven, forever serving as a priest after the order of Melchizedek. Through priesthood, the power of Godliness and His Holiness is established, it is the power and authority that God has given to all who believe in Him to act on His behalf in all things pertaining to God and His moral standard. A king is ordained to be a king as well as a priest on the throne. Through the priesthood, kings and leaders are expected to minister to God for themselves, the thrones, the people and the land (domain, kingdom, territory and nation).

Zechariah 6:12, 13

And speak unto him, saying, Thus speaketh the Lord of hosts, saying, Behold the man whose name is The Branch; and he shall grow up out of his place, and he shall build the temple of the Lord: Even he shall build the temple of the Lord; and he shall bear the glory, and shall sit and rule upon his throne; and he shall be a priest upon his throne: and the counsel of peace shall be between them both.

Priesthood is the grace to approach God, appease Him and proclaim blessing over the people and the land. Kings and leaders who understand this key spiritual principle will be able to bring God's intervention unto their territories through the power of priesthood.

9. **Power of Glory and Honour**

God has bestowed upon mankind glory and honour because He made humans in His own image, He crowned mankind with glory and honour.

Psalm 8:4-6
What is man, that thou art mindful of him? and the son of man, that thou visitest him?
For thou hast made him a little lower than the angels, and hast crowned him with glory and honour.
Thou madest him to have dominion over the works of thy hands; thou hast put all things under his feet:

Moreover, God has given kings of the earth glory and position to be honoured as His representatives on the earth to rule among the children of men, not according to their age, physical or material stature, but because of the throne and the position they occupied. That is why you see elders, aged men and women prostrates for kings who are the age of their own children. The glory and honour of a king is largely unearned. It is a bequest to the current occupant of the throne by virtue of the position and office. The crown is the glory of kings. The crown is an indication of the consecrated role of its wearer, it reflects his exalted position (Psalm 89:19-20) and indicates the presence of honour.

The Crown with glory and honour, is the potential and power to dominate the earth. That is why our Lord Jesus was crowned with thorns from the earth, the price He paid to redeem and restore the crown of earthly kings and empower kings with glory and honour to reign, rule and dominate. Unfortunately, in many nations of the world the enemy has deceived many kings and leaders to dedicate their crowns to idols and freemasonry and turn the glory of their kingdoms to whatever they worship.

10. **Power of Anointing**

Kings are to be anointed into their office by a literal anointing of oil poured on their head. The literal anointing with oil is a representation of the spiritual anointing of the Holy Spirit needed for their responsibility of leading the people or their organisations. The anointing empowers the king. When Saul was anointed, the bible say he became another man. King David was anointed by Samuel, the priest and prophet, the Spirit of the LORD came upon David from that day forward (1 Samuel 16:13). It is recorded in the Bible that God anointed David and empowers him to establish His purposes on the throne of Israel (Psalm 89). It is written that God also anointed Jesus Christ and empowers him to do well:

Acts 10:38
How God anointed Jesus of Nazareth with the Holy Spirit and with power, who went about doing good and healing all who were oppressed by the devil, for God was with Him.

Without the anointing, the king will not function at his best and his operations will be only in the natural in the wisdom of men and not in the power of God. But going by Isaiah 61, we see what a king or a leader can accomplish with the anointing.

11. **Power of Prayer with Fasting – 2 Chronicles 20, Jonah 3:5-10**

All kings and leaders need to know, understand and take advantage of their dynamic power to declare days of prayers with fasting for their domains and kingdoms to seek the face of God for divine intervention and national transformation especially in the times of trouble, calamities and uncertainties. The king of Nineveh did and God repented of the evil and calamity over the people and the land. Jehoshaphat, the king proclaimed a fast when a great multitude of armies came against him and the city of Judah.

2 Chronicles 20:3-4, 13
And Jehoshaphat feared, and set himself to seek the LORD, and proclaimed a fast throughout all Judah. And Judah gathered themselves together, to ask for help of the LORD: even out of all the cities of Judah they came to seek the LORD. And all Judah stood before the LORD, with their little ones, their wives, and their children.

King Jehoshaphat gathered the nation to seek God together. We can expect God to do great things when kings and the leaders of the people seek God. Jehoshaphat proclaimed a fast throughout Judah, he called the nation to humility and total dependence upon God through a public fast. God came through for the king and the nation. Prayer with fasting is a source of significant spiritual power because it draws us closer to the heart of God. Fasting is a powerful expression of humility before God and total dependence on God. And when the power of fasting is genuinely deployed by kings and leaders, it will bring tremendous transformation to their communities and territories. By His grace, we have led many kings and their communities through 21 to 40 days fasting and prayers for their thrones and communities which has resulted to tremendous transformation and development.

12. The Power of the Sure Mercies of David – Psalm 89:28-37

2 Samuel 7 and Psalm 89 recorded the covenant and the terms of God's covenant made with King David. One of the terms of the covenant is that God will not remove His mercy from King David and his household forever. This blessing of ongoing faithfulness and inexhaustible mercy is reflected in Isaiah 55 as "the sure mercies of David".

Isaiah 55:3-4

Incline your ear, and come unto me: hear, and your soul shall live; and I will make an everlasting covenant with you, even the sure mercies of David. Behold, I have given for a witness to the people, a leader and commander to the people.

Every king and leader of people must be wise enough to negotiate for the sure mercies of God on the throne. Nothing is as powerful as walking in divine mercy on the throne, because a throne is established by mercy (Isaiah 16:5). This is what differentiate King David from King Saul, David's predecessor as reflected in 2 Samuel 7:12-17:

"And when thy days be fulfilled, and thou shalt sleep with thy fathers, I will set up thy seed after thee, which shall proceed out of thy bowels, and I will establish his kingdom. He shall build an house

for my name, and I will stablish the throne of his kingdom for ever. I will be his father, and he shall be my son. If he commit iniquity, I will chasten him with the rod of men, and with the stripes of the children of men: but my mercy shall not depart away from him, as I took it from Saul, whom I put away before thee. And thine house and thy kingdom shall be established for ever before thee: thy throne shall be established for ever."

The family of Saul became totally extinct, but the family of David remained unto the day of Jesus Christ.

6.

MANIFESTING PRIESTHOOD ON THE THRONES

Origin and Purpose

Originally, God created mankind in His image to fellowship with Him and manifest His glory. Mankind was created with distinct moral, intellectual and spiritual capabilities. In this intent and purpose, God crowned man with glory and honour and made mankind to have dominion over the works of His hands (Psalm 8:5-9), God gave mankind a kingship and priesthood mandate to subdue and rule (Genesis 1:28). This is the foundation of the concept of Royal Priesthood, to fellowship with God and manifest His glory to creation. With the sin of Adam, mankind fell short of the glory of God and could no longer serve in this office.

Adam's sin brought in the need for redemption through sacrifice. When the tabernacle in the wilderness was erected for God to dwell with his people and the Law of Moses was instituted, the royal and priestly roles were divided. The priesthood was inaugurated with Aaron and his sons to stand before God and serve at His altar. Exodus 28 describes this priesthood. The privilege to minister to God was limited to the priests and no one apart from the priests could draw near to God. Even with this unique privilege, the priests could not come near the presence of God without proper and rigorous purification. Deuteronomy 30 outlines the mediating role of the priesthood for individuals and the nation of Israel. There and then, the fate of the nation was tied to the efficacy and faithfulness of the priesthood.

The New Priesthood

Due to the wickedness of the priests, God promised to raise a new priesthood that will do what is in the heart and mind of God.

"Then I will raise up for Myself a faithful priest who shall do

according to what is in My heart and in My mind. I will build him a sure house, and he shall walk before My anointed forever". 1 Samuel 2:35

This promise was partially fulfilled in Samuel because he functioned as a godly priest, effectively replacing the ungodly sons of Eli. It was also partially fulfilled in Zadok, in the days of David, because he replaced Eli's family line in the priesthood. The Old Testament ended on a significant promise of a king who will serve as a priest in the order of Melchizedek, a king and a priest (Psalm 110:4) and a high priest on the throne.

"And speak unto him, saying, Thus speaketh the Lord of hosts, saying, Behold the man whose name is The Branch; and he shall grow up out of his place, and he shall build the temple of the Lord: Even he shall build the temple of the Lord; and he shall bear the glory, and shall sit and rule upon his throne; and he shall be a priest upon his throne: and the counsel of peace shall be between them both". (Zechariah 6:12-13).

This kingship and priesthood mandate was fulfilled through the death and the resurrection of Jesus Christ. One of the significant torture and trials that Jesus went through was that a crown, made of thorns from the earth was forced on his head and blood came out of his head in order to redeem kings and thrones back to God. The kingship and the priesthood identity of man that was lost in the Garden of Eden through the sin of Adam was restored through Jesus once and for all. Then in Revelation 1:5-6 and 5:9-10, Jesus established and inaugurated all believers as kings and priests to rule and reign on the earth.

"And they sang a new song, saying: "You are worthy to take the scroll, And to open its seals; For You were slain, And have redeemed us to God by Your blood Out of every tribe and tongue and people and nation, And have made us kings and priests to our God; And we shall reign on the earth."

Fundamentals of Priesthood on The Thrones

- A critical spiritual principle about the priesthood on the throne is that no throne is established without a priesthood. The throne is as effective as the priesthood that ministers on the throne. This is why Jesus is the priest of God's throne in heaven, serving as our High Pries forever.
- It takes the priesthood to activate the kingship. Through priesthood, the image and holiness of God is established to draw near to God and carry His glory in order to rule and reign. Without holiness no one can appear before the LORD, you must be holy and faithful in order to be kingly. Jesus the Lamb (priest), who offered himself as a sacrifice on the cross, became Jesus the Lion of the tribe of Judah (King) through priesthood.
- Christ's redemption has made us a royal priesthood to God, no more separation between priest and kings. Throughout the history of Israel God commanded a separation between the priestly ministry and the civil leadership (kingship) of Israel. The Bible recorded the tragic story of king Uzziah who tried to function as a priest, and was stricken with leprosy until the end of his life (2 Chronicles 26). Thus, through Jesus, a king can function as a priest of God on the throne.
- Through the priesthood, kings and leaders are expected to minister to God for themselves, the thrones, the people and the land (domain, kingdom and nation). The priesthood plays the significant role of standing before God, making sacrifices (prayers) for God's people so that the nation can have peace and the people can enjoy God's blessings. Priesthood is the grace to approach God, appease Him and proclaim blessing over the people and the land.
- The throne is an altar and the priest of an altar represents God to the people and also represents the people before God. The priest is the custodian of the destiny of the people. For the strength of a throne is to the strength of the altar that is establish to service the throne and the strength of a king is to the strength of his priesthood on the throne.
- Priesthood provides the spiritual framework for effective leadership in all spheres society and the priesthood determines

the spiritual climate of every family, people and nation. In a family, when the priesthood of the father is well established it creates the spiritual atmosphere for godliness and success. God stated concerning Abraham: "For I know him, that he will command his children and his household after him, and they shall keep the way of the LORD, to do justice and judgment; that the LORD may bring upon Abraham that which he hath spoken of him". Genesis 18:19. A community or a nation is a function of the priesthood of her leaders. A faithful priesthood in every domain of influence is what is required to establish righteousness, justice and good governance.

- A fundamental understanding and restoration of the kingship and priesthood identity will empower kings and leaders to function effectively in their private life and public engagements. The priesthood functions by doing what is pleasing to God and working with integrity of heart.
- Kings and leaders in any position of authority must understand that when they stand before any false gods or idols, they are identifying their priesthood and their throne with satanic altars that will open the gates of their communities and domain of influence to satanic spirits.

Challenges of Satanic priesthood

The priest represents the people before God as well as represent God to the people in the Old Testament. Satan hijacked this principle of priesthood, leading many kings and leaders to enter into satanic covenants and to sacrifice to demons. Most traditional communities are subject to ancestral worship and sacrifices. The founding fathers of most traditional communities understood that to secure their land or territory, they needed to make covenants with supernatural powers. They made covenants with the powers of darkness and established the worship of false gods.

To worship the gods of the land, a satanic priesthood was established with powers to represent the people before those gods. The satanic altars in most communities have dedicated satanic priests apart from their king and as a matter of fact, the kings are enthroned by the priests through demonic sacrifices, rites of enthronement, oaths and dedication. The satanic priesthood remains a stronghold over many peoples and nations. It brings a covering of darkness over the people and the territory, and makes even the kings to rebel against God.

Alas, the major challenge to any king or leader especially in the traditional setting is ancestral worship, sacrifices to idols or other forms of satanic priesthood. It does not matter whether you profess as a Christian or not. Through the rites of enthronement, kings are made to enter into covenant with the powers of darkness to fortify themselves with evil or ancestral powers to be strong to rule. Through the priestly enthronement, the kings are made to become the custodian of the idols of the land and to worship other gods, many times against their conscience. In fact, fidelity to the royal priesthood of Jesus Christ and rejection of kingly obligations that seek to traverse it is met with great opposition and sometimes may lead to major chaos in many communities.

During the enthronement of a certain monarch, as part of the rites, the king was obliged to choose a guardian idol that he will be worshipping when he ascends the throne. During his coronation, the king was asked by his community elders to choose which of the lesser gods he will worship after he has been crowned as their king. The monarch being a Christian, told the community of elders that now that he is the king on the throne, he has an understanding that he is above the lesser gods that have not made the heaven and the earth, but as a priest and a king on the throne he will represent the people before the Almighty God in the name of Jesus Christ and not through other lesser gods. The Christian king's decision and declaration prevailed and overruled the tradition of idolatry in that community. Many times, it takes courage, boldness and the wisdom of God to overcome the challenges on the throne.

Challenges of Religious Priesthood

Society is still subject to religious priesthood, a priesthood of ceremonial worship that existed in the times of Jesus Christ. Our Lord and Saviour Jesus Christ had the greatest confrontations with the religious leaders of His day. Matthew 23 and Mark 7 detailed the characteristics of religious priesthood:

- A form of priesthood that honours God with their lips, but their

heir heart is far from God.

- A priesthood that set aside the commandments of God, but hold on to the traditions of the elders.
- A priesthood that has a form of godliness, but lacks the power of God.
- A priesthood that makes the word of God of no effect.
- A priesthood that creates a divide between the clergy and the laity.
- A priesthood that still separates the priestly ministry from the kingly authority, establishment of separation between the church and the state.
- A priesthood that establishes religious syncretism.

Religious priesthood described above presents great challenges to kings because they promote a gospel that does not object to kingly obligations that traverse the fidelity of godly priesthood. Also, in this construct, kings are not taught that they too are ministers of God on their thrones.

Manifesting Priesthood on the throne

Most kings, leaders in corporate world and marketplaces as well as political government know about exercising authority on the thrones, but many do not know about the power of manifesting their priesthood on the thrones; while others subscribe to satanic priesthood to fortify themselves in order to ward off attacks and challenges on their thrones or to empower themselves to do wickedness.

- The first principle of manifesting priesthood on the throne is establishing the altar of God on the throne. This has to be done through repentance and atonements for the sins on the throne (past and present), making a covenant with God and dedicating their thrones to God. We have been involved in helping many kings and leaders to dedicate their thrones to God in many parts of Africa.
- The second principle of manifesting priesthood on the throne is sacrifice, it is sacrifice that produces power. This has to be done by the king presenting himself as a living sacrifice unto God Almighty, offerings prayers and thanksgiving unto God daily.

Presenting his throne, offering prayers for the people and the community and blessing the land. Prayer is the breath and life of Priesthood.

- The third principle of manifesting priesthood on the throne is to lead the entire community into covenant with God after a period of not less than twenty-one days prayers and fasting in the land, and afterwards to open the house of God in the palace and establish 24/7 prayers in the palace.
- King David brought the ark of God into Jerusalem, which is detailed in 1 Chronicles 15 and 16. The ark of God represented the presence and the glory of God in Israel. Bringing the ark of God is bringing the presence of God. King David had a heart for God and the house of the LORD. King David understood the importance and the blessings of dwelling in the presence of God and providing a place of worship for God.
- To manifest priesthood on the throne is to always seek the LORD for counsels before taking any major decision. It is recorded in Joshua 9 how Joshua and the leaders of Israel were deceived by the Gibeonites because they did not ask counsel of the LORD. Joshua and the leaders of Israel relied only on what they could see, but never sought the LORD. King David always asked counsels from the LORD from the priest before taking any major decision. Even though the priesthood was separated from the kingship in his time, King David always asked a priest for the ephod in order to discern the mind of God and receive counsels from the LORD. Today, there is no separation between the priesthood and the kingship, but kings and leaders must manifest priesthood on their thrones by spending time with God and open their hearts to God's counsel.

7.

THE DESIGN AND PURPOSE OF THRONES

God and the Earthly Thrones

Kings and all people in authority must bear in mind, they are sitting on the throne of the Lord as God's representative and therefore, their first allegiance must be to God: for the Lord subjects leaders to greater punishment should they fail to fulfil His purpose on the throne. Then Solomon sat on the throne of the LORD as king instead of David his father, and prospered; and all Israel obeyed him (1 Chron. 29:23).

The Design of Thrones

Thrones are designed by God to be the throne of glory:

> *He raiseth up the poor out of the dust, and lifteth up the beggar from the dunghill, to set them among princes, and to make them inherit the throne of glory: for the pillars of the earth are the LORD'S, and he hath set the world upon them (1 Sam. 2:8).*

The throne of glory is the design of God for the manifestations of the Sons of God to establish His purpose on the earth.

The King and the Throne

The king and the throne are two separate entities, the throne is not just the chair where royalty sit, it is a representation of the power of the dignitary who sits on it and sometimes confer that power. The throne actually is what distinguish the king and should not be taken lightly because kings derive their power, authority and influence from the identity of their thrones. However, the identity of the throne is subject to its history, foundations, geographical spread and many other factors.

God enthroned Adam in the Garden of Eden, and gave him authority over the fullness of the land and the kingdom (Genesis 2:16-20). Pharaoh enthroned Joseph as ruler over his kingdom: And Pharaoh said unto Joseph, Forasmuch as God hath shewed thee all this, there is none so discreet and wise as thou art: Thou shalt be over my house, and according unto thy word shall all my people be ruled: only in the throne will I be greater than thou. And Pharaoh said unto Joseph, See, I have set thee over all the land of Egypt (Genesis 41:39-41).

Kings, Rulers, Leaders and Governments are Actually Ministers of God

One day the Bishop of the Anglican Communion and I visited the paramount king of his city to pray with him. In the palace was this big Bible on the table before the king that perhaps has not been opened for a while and being led by His Spirit, I requested the queen to assist the king to open to Romans 13:1-4:

> *Let every soul be subject unto the higher powers. For there is no power but of God: the powers that be are ordained of God. Whosoever therefore resisteth the power, resisteth the ordinance of God: and they that resist shall receive to themselves damnation. For rulers are not a terror to good works, but to the evil. Wilt thou then not be afraid of the power? do that which is good, and thou shalt have praise of the same: For he is the minister of God to thee for good. But if thou do that which is evil, be afraid; for he beareth not the sword in vain: for he is the minister of God, a revenger to execute wrath upon him that doeth evil.*

After reading the scripture, I asked the king this question: 'Your royal majesty, should any major disaster (God forbid) come upon this city, where will the people run to for help – the bishop or himself?' He replied that the people will run to him. I then told the king that he needed more anointing than even the bishop and that as a matter of fact, he the king is a minister of God ordained by God on the throne for the whole kingdom. The king and the queen by his side exclaimed that no one has ever told them that they are ministers of God on the throne as they are only referred to as traditional leaders. Their countenances changed for their understanding was enlightened that not only religious leaders are ministers of God, but kings are ministers of God and that such position carry great responsibility towards God first and foremost.

Thrones Have Foundations

Thrones have foundations and these foundations affect and influence the activities, decisions and lifestyles of those who sit on the thrones. God's Throne has foundations and the foundations are described to be righteousness and justice. What always proceed from His Throne are mercy and truth. The LORD reigns; let the earth rejoice; let the multitude of isles be glad thereof. Clouds and darkness are round about him: righteousness and judgment are the habitation of his throne (Psalms 97:1 -2).

> *Justice and judgment are the habitation of thy throne: mercy and truth shall go before thy face* (Psalms 89:14)

Unfortunately, the foundations of most thrones are not founded on righteousness and justice, but founded on idolatry, freemasonry, occultism and human philosophies and ideologies which makes most kings and people in authority not to serve God with a perfect heart most of the time. This dynamic of thrones is further explained in chapter nineteen of this book.

Foundations of Earthly Thrones Must be Redeemed

As a king may be guilty of sins to the detriment of the nation, so also the thrones may be adjured guilty which may bring serious hardship on the land and the people:

> *And the woman of Tekoah said unto the king, My lord, O king, the iniquity be on me, and on my father's house: and the king and his throne be guiltless.* 2 Samuel 14:9

The burden of redeeming thrones and throne's cleansing in order to redeem the land and release nations into their redemptive purposes must include practical strategies of cleansing the thrones of past sins and evil practices as part of the throne paradigm. The cleansing of thrones, the breaking of traditional occult bondages of nations must be understood as a key step in the process of step by step, kingdom by kingdom, of releasing the nations out of foundations of thrones that produces wicked rulers and bad leadership, dealing with foundations that promotes Satanic policies against God's principles and purposes amongst the nations.

This means that even in certain cases, where ancient kingdoms no longer exist, where old, ancient thrones and royal houses were established before but no longer exist, the occult bondages are still in place constituting a major blockage of the redemption of the land, the resources of the people, the purposes of God and there must be diligent spiritual mapping and cleansing of such ancient thrones and gates in the land.

The Purpose of the Throne

It is said that when you do not know the purpose of a thing, you will definitely abuse it. The same is true for thrones and all position of power, influence, authority and leadership be it household, religious settings, business and corporate world, and government. The main purpose of thrones is to administer judgement and justice.

Blessed be the LORD thy God, which delighted in thee, to set thee on the throne of Israel: because the LORD loved Israel for ever, therefore made he thee king, to do judgment and justice (1 Kings 10:9).

God gave Solomon a throne over Israel to give judgement and justice. Two women brought a baby to the king, both of them claimed to be the mother. King Solomon told them to cut the baby in half and give each woman half part of the baby using the wisdom of the overwhelming maternity instinct to reveal the true mother of the child. The baby given back to the true mother is the justice. The king of another kingdom shared his testimony with me of a case of theft that was brought to the king's court by two people who claimed ownership of a herd of sheep. The king himself, a well-respected lawyer who has trained many lawyers said he requested the herd of sheep be brought and locked up in a room in the king's court while he went to the inner chamber and knelt down to pray to God for wisdom to administer justice.

In his spirit he heard the word, my sheep hear my voice and they follow me. Next day, he summoned all concerned to the king's court to deliver his judgement and requested the two people who claimed ownership to come forward. He asked the first one to go and talk to the sheep, he went and nothing happened and the second person was asked to go and do the same. At the voice of the second person, the sheep started making noise and running around the room. Of course, the herd of sheep was released to the true owner. No ambiguity in the judgment.

The Throne is a Place of Strategy

The throne is a place of strategies, not a place of manipulation and mischief. A place to download blueprints, develop productive plans and implement strategies to develop the land and nation. For people to be significantly successful on the thrones, they need to obtain wisdom, counsels and strategies from God. Every day, the land and the nations are faced with challenges and many things demanding attention and solutions that requires beyond the ordinary and fresh strategies to proffer solution headlong. Joseph developed and implemented fourteen years strategies to rescue Egypt from famine by the wisdom of God.

The Throne is Operated by the Sceptre of Righteousness

Thy throne, O God, is for ever and ever: a sceptre of righteousness is the sceptre of Your kingdom. You love righteousness, and hate wickedness: therefore God, Your God, has anointed thee with the oil of gladness above thy fellows (Psalm 45:6, 7 and Heb. 1:8).

A sceptre is an ornamental rod or staff borne by rulers as an emblem of authority. Beyond that the sceptre of righteousness is to embrace righteous behaviour, conduct and enforce righteous behaviour as a ruler or head of any organisation, workplace, and government. It is to love righteousness and develop hatred for evil and wickedness in whatever position you find yourself, most especially in the marketplaces and government. It is the ability to govern righteously and enforce righteous behaviour. Clearly God is distressed by the lack of righteousness in His churches and in the governments of the nations. Before you take up throne assignment, you must settle with God to unite your heart to fear Him and to do what is right and be committed to the oath of office.

The Throne is the Centre of Worship

Every kingdom is created by God to worship God. The purpose of a king is to influence worship in his domain, kingdom and to bring glory to God. Kings have the God-given mandate, assignment and service to decree and command duties of worship of God and bringing thanksgiving to God. (2 Sam. 6; 1 Chron. 15). That is why the enemy deceives leaders of many kingdoms and nations into the worship of other objects that is not the God of heaven and earth. A kingdom is as strong as its worship of the true God and the heart of a kingdom is determined by the heart of the king's worship to God. King David's worship pulled his kingdom from poverty, disunity, ethnic hatred, and reproach.

This created an atmosphere for the defeat of their enemies, the restoration of the ark of the covenant of the Lord of the whole earth, social justice and development. Almost every time a good king gets to the throne or discovers the greatness of God, the first thing they do is to open the house of God for worship, remove idolatry from the throne and the land, establish a covenant with God, the people and the land; and restore the true worship. This is the pragmatic process of drawing eternal and sustainable blessings of God upon the land to many generations.

The Throne Determines the Destiny of a Nation

We all know that leaders determine the destiny of their nations and the bible put it bluntly in Ecclesiastes 10:16, 17:

"Happy is that land (nation) when their king/leader is of noble character and their officials feast at the proper time for strength and not for drunkenness. But woe to the land (nation) when their king is a child and their officials feast in the morning."

It is also written: "**when the righteous are in authority, the people rejoice: but when the wicked beareth rule, the people mourn.**" Proverbs 29:2 . It is to the benefit of a community or a nation when the righteous rules or govern, but when the wicked rules lawlessness, corruption, mischiefs and oppressions increases.

8.

FUNDAMENTALS AND DYNAMICS OF THRONES

Transforming communities and nations can never be accomplished without raising kings, queens, rulers and leaders with impeccable characters and building thrones with the right foundations capable of sustaining development, godly government and good governance. However, to accomplish these tasks we need to understand the fundamentals of thrones and we need to take a good look at the spiritual dynamics of thrones.

Fundamentals of Thrones
The following constitutes the crucial fundamentals of thrones that we need to take into consideration in order to establish good governance among the nations:

1. Fundamentally, we need to understand that all positions of power, authority and influence where decisions are made that affects others are thrones. That is why all other purposes are subject to the thrones – government, unity, reformation, transformation, rebuilding, establishing righteousness and justice, dealing with the wicked of the land and becoming a voice for the poor and the needy. Good governance must encompass all domains of influence in any given territory, society or nation. Failure at any level, be it at the family level will impact negatively on good governance in the society.

2. The fact that you occupy the position of power, authority or influence does not mean you can operate on the throne successfully. Throne assignment and leadership mandate is not an easy task. If you have not developed the noble character for the throne, you can be sure that your leadership will be a disaster because the throne will reveal your character. You need the right training that will build your capacity to operate on the throne –

Daniel 1:3-4. The throne's training and mentorship must be intentionally programmed into our fabrics of life from birth, in our families and all institutions.

3. Whereas thrones are redemptive tools and God's infrastructure of government and governance we need to know that the enemy guard jealously over the thrones and will contend fiercely when you begin to deal with thrones. That is why the battle for the throne is a fierce battle in most communities and nations. The battle for thrones most of the time bring chaos and bloodshed in the nation. The throne is contentious in any domain of influence.

4. We need to understand that the throne controls the traditions, the customs and culture of most territories especially the traditional communities. Therefore, possessing the gates of the thrones is a fundamental strategy to deal with occult bondages, idolatry, traditions and corruption in any community in order to establish godly government and governance. This is not an easy challenge in most traditional communities.

5. Every throne has a redemptive purpose. The throne is a dynamic representation and extension of the Throne of God to establish His purposes everywhere on earth. The king or leader must discover and be prepared to fulfil God's redemptive purpose for the throne in order to be a blessing to the people. No throne is small, every throne is strategic for God's redemptive purpose. God can make a throne great, enlarge the scope and borders of a king on a throne based on the king's covenant with God on the throne and ability to fulfil God's purpose on the throne (Luke 1:32, 33).

6. We need to know that there are thrones of iniquity and we need to know how to deal with the thrones of iniquity (Psalm 94:20-23), thrones of the wicked (2 Kings 11) and satan's thrones in any given territory. This will require developing actionable plans and implement strategies to overthrow the thrones of wickedness and develop the skills to establish righteous thrones. This is covered extensively in Chapter Twenty of this book.

7. Another fundamental of throne is that all the thrones belong to God. That is why it is recorded that Solomon sat on the throne of God instead of his father David – 1 Chronicles. 29:23; to this extent, God expect everyone who sits on the throne to fear Him, to seek His face for wisdom and counsel in order to establish

righteousness and justice on the throne.

Dynamics of Thrones

The thrones consist of complex dynamics that affect the leader, the throne and their organisation or nation. Here we posit two major dynamics of thrones that we need to look into in order to address the issues of bad leadership and bad governance in every domain of influence.

1. The King or Leader Who Sits on The Throne Is an Entity on His/Her Own with Many Complex Dynamics

The personality that sits in the position of leadership in any organisation or domain of influence is a determinant factor in the way the organisation will go, and this personality is subject to many patterns that influence his/her leadership. The heart of the king or leader is subject to many complex dynamics and what plays out from the heart of kings and leaders affects their decisions and the way the people, the organisation or the nation will go.

The dynamics must be factored into kingship and leadership development, which is why God chose David and described him as a man after His own heart. Saul was the first God-appointed King of Israel. He looked and acted the part. He was known for his courage and generosity. He was tall and striking in appearance. At first, Saul did well. But it did not take long for his pride to grow and his reliance on God to fade. King Saul was rejected from being a king because of his disobedience. Then, God sent His prophet Samuel to Saul: *"But now your kingdom shall not endure. The Lord has sought for Himself a man after His own heart, and the Lord has appointed him ruler over His people, because you have not kept what the Lord commanded you."* (1 Samuel 13:14).

Afterwards, Samuel was instructed to go to the house of Jesse, the father of David to go and anoint a king for Israel. When Samuel got there, he was about to anoint Eliab, the firstborn of Jesse, but the Lord refused him. But the Lord said to Samuel, *"Do not look at his appearance or at his physical stature, because I have refused him. For the Lord does not see as man sees; for man looks at the outward appearance, but the Lord looks at the heart."* (1 Samuel

16:7). Jeremiah 17:10 says: "*I the Lord search the heart and examine the mind, to reward each person according to their conduct, according to what their deeds deserve.*"

Why God does looks at the heart? The heart is subject to many complex dynamics, it is subject to deception, wickedness and pride if it is not totally committed to the fear of God. King David had this testimony written concerning him: "*So David shepherded them according to the integrity of his heart...*" (Psalm 78:72). This indicated that King David's heart has been trained in the art of integrity. Today, integrity of heart is still a major issue in the lives of many people in leadership positions, whereas integrity of heart remains a basic ingredient for national transformation and sustainable development. We need leaders with impeccable character. The Bible put it bluntly in Ecclesiastes 10:16, 17:

"Happy is that land (nation) when their king/leader is of noble character and their officials feast at the proper time for strength and not for drunkenness. But woe to the land (nation) when their king is a child and their officials feast in the morning."

The power of influence is strong. We need people whose heart are exercised in integrity in positions of leadership. We need leaders whose heart are established in the fear of God.

"And Rehoboam did evil because he did not set his heart to seek the LORD..". 2 Chro. 12:14

A leader whose heart is NOT prepared in advance for his/her throne assignment will become an instrument of wickedness and bad leadership when they get to the throne. Another complex dynamic of the king is the king's identity. The concept of identity is a complex one, shaped by individual characteristics, family dynamics, historical factors, and social and political contexts. Who am I? Many kings and people in position of leadership suffer from identity crisis. The concept typically refers to questioning your place in the world and who you are as a person.

Maybe you feel you're no longer connected to a purpose which causes confusion, depression, insecurity and instability. When a leader or a king is insecure, it does not mean weakness but such a leader become dangerous to the organisation or nation. Saul was such a leader; he admitted to Samuel, "I feared the people and obeyed their voice." (1 Samuel 15:24). Saul was always concerned about how the people saw him and whether he had acceptance with them or not. Moreover, another complex dynamic is when a king or a leader does not know the purpose of the throne. I have seen many kings and leaders ascend the throne without a clear understanding of the purpose of thrones.

And when the purpose of a thing is not known, abuse is inevitable. I had the privilege of interviewing a prince before he was selected and enthroned as the king over his community. I asked him what he is going to do if he becomes the king and whether he understand the challenges that awaits him. All he said was that he is a prince and that one day he knows he is entitled to the throne and could become the king.

2. On the other hand, a throne by itself is also an entity with complex dynamics

Thrones have foundations and the foundations influence the one who sits on the throne, it may be positive and may be negative; but the influence of the foundations of thrones on the person that sit on the throne and subsequently the people, the community and the nation cannot be ignored. Jeroboam, the son of Nebat became the first king of the divided northern kingdom of Israel. Though Jeroboam began well, he did not end well. He established an unprecedented foundation of idolatry on the throne. He had two golden calves made for the people to worship in the northern kingdom and made Israel to sin. This evil foundation of idolatry is often referred to as "the sins of Jeroboam, the son of Nebat" in later chapters of 1 and 2 Kings.

God raised him up as a king, yet as king he plunged the entire nation into sin. What happened after him was that almost every king that reigned after him, the Bible showed that even they started well, they did not depart from the sin of Jeroboam the son of Nebat who taught Israel to sin. The foundation he laid became a stumbling block to most kings after him.

The evil foundation he laid on the throne offers an example of the powerful influence an evil foundation upon a throne can have over other kings in succession in a negative way. In contemporary life, we ministered to so many kings who ten years of their reign witnessed so many setbacks even though they have the mind of doing what is right, but they confessed they were hindered until we redeemed the thrones. In government and politics, we have trained political leaders who confessed that they don't understand what has hindered them for the many years they have been in government until they came about this knowledge.

A write-up by Reuben Abati in *Guardian Newspaper* of 14 October 2016 caught my attention. Here is the excerpt of what he wrote:

"People tend to be alarmed when the Nigerian Presidency takes certain decisions. They don't think the decision makes sense. Sometimes, they wonder if something has not gone wrong with the thinking process at that highest level of the country. I have heard people insist that there is some form of witchcraft at work in the country's seat of government. I am ordinarily not a superstitious person, but working in the Villa, I eventually became convinced that there must be something supernatural about power and closeness to it. I'll start with a personal testimony. I was given an apartment to live in inside the Villa. It was furnished and equipped. But when my son, Michael arrived, one of my brothers came with a pastor who was supposed to stay in the apartment. But the man refused claiming that the Villa was full of evil spirits and that there would soon be a fire accident in the apartment. He complained about too much human sacrifice around the Villa and advised that my family must never sleep overnight inside the Villa. I thought the man was talking nonsense and he wanted the luxury of a hotel accommodation. But he turned out to be right. The day I hosted family friends in that apartment and they slept overnight, there was indeed a fire accident. The guests escaped and they were so thankful. Not long after, the President's physician living two compounds away had a fire accident in his home. He and his children could have died. He escaped with bruises. Around the Villa while I was there, someone always died or their relations died. I can confirm that every principal officer suffered one tragedy or the other; it was as if you needed to sacrifice something to remain on duty inside that environment. .... I really don't envy the people who work in Aso Villa, the seat of Nigeria's Presidency. For about six months, I couldn't even breathe properly. For another

two months, I was on crutches. But I considered myself far luckier than the others who were either nursing a terminal disease or who could not get it up..... When Presidents make mistakes, they are probably victims of a force higher than what we can imagine. Every student of Aso Villa politics would readily admit that when people get in there, they actually become something else. They act like they are under a spell. When you issue a well- crafted statement, the public accepts it wrongly. When the President makes a speech and he truly means well, the speech is interpreted wrongly by the public. When a policy is introduced, somehow, something just goes wrong.... Since Buhari government assumed office, it has been one mistake after another. Those mistakes don't look normal, the same way they didn't look normal under President Jonathan. I am therefore convinced that there is an evil spell enveloping this country. We need to rescue Nigeria from the forces of darkness ...

The conclusion by the writer that we need to rescue the throne of government and governance is right, and this is applicable to the seat of government of many nations. In another nation, the president abandoned the government house and called on the ministers of God to pray and drive away evil spirits from the state house. Many people are totally oblivious of the challenges that kings and leaders are facing because of evil foundations. A particular king was brought to my office for prayers. The battle to terminate his life was so intense because he and the queen refused to worship the idols of the land. His vehicle was grounded and resources went down mysteriously. For two years he suffered several attacks and was sick to the point of death, yet doctors diagnosed nothing.

As a matter of fact, it was his personal physician that eventually brought him to the office for ministration. According to the king, he had fasted many days and months to deal with his problems to no avail and tried everything medically as well, yet no major improvement. He loves the Lord and has made up his mind to do the will of God on the throne but, now he cannot understand or explain why he had to pass through terrible experiences and sickness that no one can diagnose. He told me how he used to hear the sound of footsteps in and around his palace in the night, but he would not see anybody no matter how much he searched. Sometimes, he would shout "who are you?" but, no one will answer only that the footsteps will continue. He experienced series of terrible things like this and he said to me that he did know he could still be alive.

Briefly, I explained to him the basic principles of the foundations of the throne and the impact on the king and I said to the king, "Your Royal Highness; the footsteps you hear are voices from the foundations of the throne you are sitting upon because of the ancestral dedication of the throne to the powers of darkness and that he is a tenant in the palace until they are dealt with spiritually." Based on the principles presented in this book, we ministered to him and his health was restored. Afterwards, the king proclaimed a 40 days prayer and fasting in the palace where all the pastors and minsters of the kingdom gathered together daily to pray and seek the face of God for the throne and the kingdom. In the course of praying for the kingdom, we carried out the process of redeeming the throne. In the palace, there was room called 'the king's strong room' where the king could disappear at will, (perhaps as they say, to commune with the ancestors) or to incubate himself in time of war to receive power to wage war against his enemies.

In this room located strategically in the palace, there were no windows, no light, the walls and ground not plastered. No one but the king must enter into it. The room contained the major idols of the land that the ancestors had worshipped for years before he came to the throne. Since he became king, he had never entered the room once and had not bothered himself about the room since he is a Christian. After prayers and seeking the face of God, we led the king to entrance of the room and led him into proper repentance and atonement for the ancestral sins of idolatry of the land and throne. He renounced all the covenant of the land with powers of darkness. Thereafter, we opened the room and within two hours brought out all the gods and idolatrous articles and vessels on after the other. The king at first did not want us to enter the room for fear that something evil will happen to us but, we assured him nothing will happen.

When we finished, it was the king himself that set them on fire with praises to God. The said, he would renovate the room to either make it a library or prayer closet. The king dedicated himself, the throne and his palace to the true and living God and till date, the king and the community are enjoying unprecedented social and economic growth.

Today, the king is not ashamed to share his testimony of how God delivered him, his throne and kingdom from the shackles and bondage of satanic foundation and afterwards, the peace and prosperity of the kingdom. Another critical and complex dynamic of thrones is that a throne as an entity may be guilty of iniquity. The sin of a king or a leader on the throne is not a personal sin, but a national sin. After the death of King Saul, David a man after God's own heart was enthroned king over Israel. The nation was expecting great blessings now that there is a righteous king on the throne, but the nation was plagued with famine:

"Now there was a famine in the days of David for three years, year after year; and David inquired of the Lord. And the Lord answered, "It is because of Saul and his bloodthirsty house, because he killed the Gibeonites." So the king called the Gibeonites and spoke to them. Now the Gibeonites were not of the children of Israel, but of the remnant of the Amorites; the children of Israel had sworn protection to them, but Saul had sought to kill them in his zeal for the children of Israel and Judah. Therefore David said to the Gibeonites, "What shall I do for you? And with what shall I make atonement that you may bless the inheritance of the Lord?" (2 Samuel 21:1-6).*

Until the issue of the sin of King Saul, the predecessor of King David was properly addressed, the nation did not make any progress. The wisdom behind this dynamic is that we may need to seek strategies from God to redeem thrones so that kings, people in authority can fulfil their redemptive purpose for the nations. Again, the throne and every leadership position attract vicious envy and jealousy, betrayal and manipulations as well as bloodshed.

Absalom is best known for his betrayal of his father King David. He thought he could rule the country better than his father; he instituted a rebellion that almost ruined the reign of King David (2 Samuel 16-17). Moreover, as stated in earlier chapter; a throne is not only about the king or the leader. It comprises of other key players around the throne that influences the king, decision making and policy implementation. This is a complex dynamic, because for a reign of righteousness the king as well as the princes must rule with justice.

"Behold, a king will reign in righteousness, And princes will rule with justice. A man will be as a hiding place from the wind, And a cover from the tempest, As rivers of water in a dry place, As the shadow of a great rock in a weary land." Isaiah 32:1-2

A beneficent government and governance is established when the king and nobles alike are endowed with the virtues and character necessary for their office and purpose on the throne.

Conclusion

In concluding this chapter, we need to understand the complex dynamics of thrones to guide us in the process of raising leaders and establishing righteousness on the thrones. We need to understand that the establishment of idolatry, occultism, freemasonry and satanic covenants have done a lot to secure the foundations of many thrones to the devil, wickedness and all forms demonic ideologies, wicked traditions and culture. Therefore, we have to arise everywhere to join hands together locally and globally to address these issues in order to establish righteousness, justice and good governance.

9.

THE THRONE OF THE HEART

And thou, Solomon my son, know thou the God of thy father, and: if thou seek him, he will be found of thee; but if thou forsake him, serve him with a perfect heart and with a willing mind: for the Lord searcheth all hearts, and understandeth all the imaginations of the thoughts: if you seek him, he will be found of thee; but if thou forsake him, he will cast thee off for ever. 1 Chronicles 28:9

The heart is the most important part of a thing that is why it is said, the heart of the matter is the matter of the heart. The heart is the seat of life, emotion and our being. All we are, do and our entire make up is a function of the state of our hearts. In most cases, the heart is used in many ways to describe who a person is or how a person conducts himself or herself. You hear expressions such as: "lion-hearted", "chicken-hearted", depicting bravery and cowardice respectively. Further expression, "his heart is in the right place" or "his heart is not in it", "tender-hearted", "the man or woman is heartless", "in one's heart of heart", "largeness of heart", demonstrate through language and expression the primacy and importance of the and heart and its condition.

With the knowledge and understanding that the 'heart' represents who we are, what we do, how we conduct our lives, it is no wonder that in searching for a king for Israel, God prepared for Himself David, a man after His own heart; for He does not look at physical appearance but, He searches the heart. Therefore, the state of our heart is very significant in everything we do especially our leadership mandate and assignment. There is one 'throne' that matters more than any other throne and that is the throne of your heart. It is a great mystery that, God has chosen not to dwell in any building made of hands, but to make us as living stones and His dwelling place. Our hearts, His Throne is a great mystery.

Here is one throne that matters more than any other throne because

God created your heart as the seat of His authority in your life where he can direct your paths and order your steps as well as reign and govern through you. The amazing thing about God is even though he is all-powerful he will not force himself onto the throne of your heart. Whoever sits on the throne of your heart is who you worship and serve. Scripture tells us where our treasure is, that is also where our heart is and you are encouraged to allow God to sit on the throne of your heart. 1 Peter 3:15 "...*but sanctity (make holy, pure) Christ as Lord in your hearts*..." Put Christ first! Put Him on the throne of your hearts!

Fundamentals of the Throne of God in our Hearts

- God has chosen not to dwell in any building made of hands, but to make us as living stones and His dwelling place.
- In every heart, there is a throne and that throne must be wholly dedicated to God.
- The throne of your heart has room for only one king.
- This throne can be taken over by different things apart from God who created it and that amounts to rebellion against God.
- Whoever is seated on the throne of your heart will determine who reigns in your life.
- You have a choice to whom you give and dedicate the throne of your heart to.
- Whatever is on the throne of your heart is what you will worship.
- You need to examine the reins of your heart to ascertain what are the things that determine what you worship, what gives you joy and what influences your decision-making processes.

Proverbs 11:20
They that are of a froward heart are abomination to the LORD: but such as are upright in their way are his delight.

You Cannot Serve Two Masters

Too often, we find out that two natures are contending and two principles struggling for sovereignty in our hearts. Our hearts are apt to be divided between two counsels, opinions and intentions: between good and evil. A man of divided heart is weak and will cause more harm than good especially when it comes to operating on the thrones and taking far-reaching decisions that can affect the destinies of many generations afterwards.

Matthew 6: 21, 24
For where your treasure is, there will your heart be also.
No man can serve two masters: for either he will hate the one,
and love the other; or else he will hold to the one, and despise the
other. Ye cannot serve God and mammon.

The Conditions of the Heart

Jeremiah, the prophet testifies to the conditions of every human heart in the Book of Law (Jeremiah 17:9, 10).

Jeremiah 17: 9, 10
"The heart is deceitful above all things, and desperately wicked;
Who can know it? I, the LORD, search the heart, I test the mind,
even to give every man according to his ways, according to the fruit
of his doings."

There is a problem of the heart that needs to be dealt with, to be fixed – the heart is deceitful above all things and desperately wicked. For a person to be and do what is right – he must have integrity established in his heart. If a person's heart is not right, that person cannot be honest and trustworthy. In order for a leader to bring sustainable transformation, the heart must be right and established with integrity. All matters of Godly government and good governance rest on this principle.

The constitution of the nation may be good and the system or structure of government excellent, however, if the executors are not established in integrity, the nation or government cannot be administered properly. In leadership and the operating principles on the thrones, the heart constitutes a serious factor. No matter how spiritual a person is, without integrity of heart, he will not lead transformation successfully. Jeremiah's thesis is about the natural state of the heart. It shows that the heart is not neutral, static or indifferent and this assessment of the heart is God's verdict. It shows the heart to be actively and unreservedly evil, whose only solution is total and continuous submission to God.

What is the State of Your Heart?

- The heart is susceptible to deception. You must understand that we possess a boundless ability to deceive ourselves and be deceived. This condition of the heart's susceptibility to deception if not properly dealt with will eventually bring dire consequences.
- The heart is susceptible to desperate wickedness.

Matthew 15:19, 20
For out of the heart proceed evil thoughts, murders, adulteries, fornications, thefts, false witness, and blasphemies:
These are the things which defile a man: but to eat with unwashen hands defileth not a man

The Solution to the Grave Conditions of the Heart

The heart is deceitful and desperately wicked, but the good news is that God who created our heart can help us if we turn unto Him wholeheartedly for help. He can tighten, strengthen, knit our hearts, fasten our hearts and give us singleness of heart by His grace and mercy and make us strong to choose good and reject evil in order to enforce His reign and the supremacy of His kingdom in our sphere of influence and thrones. King David, a man after God's heart is a good example when it comes to turning one's heart unto God. He understood from the beginning that God searches the heart.

All the time David will always cry to God for help:

Psalm 86:11.12
*Teach me Your way, O LORD, I will walk in Your truth, **unite my heart to fear Your name.** I will praise You, O Lord my God, with all my heart,and I will glorify Your name forevermore*

Psalm 119:36-38
Incline my heart to Your testimonies, *and not to covetousness. Turn away my eyes from looking at worthless things and revive me in Your*

Unite my heart to fear Your name, the contemporary word for unite include to join, solidify, strengthen, merge, band together, become one, blend, mix, interpenetrate, entwine, intertwine, gather together, tighten and fasten. Incline my heart, the contemporary word incline includes to turn, prepare, bend, conduct, tend.

Largeness of Heart – 1 King 4:29

The largeness of heart is a crucial condition of a leader's heart. It is another fundamental principle of operating on the thrones. King Solomon, although not a standard character on marriage but a standard character on management of God's people. Competent at managing fully equipped with two operating principles: wisdom and largeness of heart You find Solomon's request for wisdom above all things in 1Kings 3: 7-9. Wisdom – Basic principle in management, knowledge is not enough wisdom is extraordinary ability to solve problems. Largeness of heart even as the sand of the seashore – beyond the boundary of the sea. Largeness of heart is about inclusion and diversity. Everyone with a small heart is a foolish person, he does not have the mind of God. Pride is a manifestation of foolishness – a product of narrow-mindedness, not seeing the bigger picture and not seeing God's perspective. It is very hard if not impossible for a person with a large heart to be proud.

Pride is an indication that a person's heart is narrow, deceitful and wicked. Kings, leaders and everyone who manages God's people need much wisdom and largeness of heart. The secret of humility and wisdom is to fear God and to have a large heart. When many matters are poorly managed or handled, you may attribute the cause to foolishness, but the root of foolishness or incompetence comes from a narrow heart. Pray and ask for a large heart and you will become a person of wisdom and become the leader God intended you to be. The largeness of heart helps to solve many problems and challenges you will face in any leadership position.

The largeness of heart does not mean to be loose or weak, you are strict and disciplined with yourself and great values, yet your heart towards others is large. You will have the capacity to accommodate people from diverse orientations, backgrounds and ethnics yet without prejudice or hatred, not feeling inferior nor superior to others. Again, largeness of heart has to do with honesty in the heart, not the absence of lying and cheating alone but Truthfulness and genuineness. Moreover, the ability to readily and totally forgive offenders and forget has to do with the largeness of heart – a heart after the heart of God. Indeed, we need an abundance of grace and breakthrough when it comes to obtaining and cultivating largeness of heart in order to establish good governance.

The Importance of the Heart in Leadership and Operating on the Thrones

The most significant leadership tool you have is your heart. Knowing what it is and how to use it is the key to leadership effectiveness. We cannot over emphasize the critical position of the heart in leadership and to operate on the thrones because the heart is the centre of leadership. That is why when God is looking for a king, he searches for those whose heart is after His own heart.

*Acts 13:22 – **A Heart After God's Heart***
"After removing Saul, he made David their king. He testified concerning him: 'I have found David the son of Jesse, a man after My own heart; who will do all My will.'

Great leaders are those who are strong and decisive but also humble who lead by the integrity of their hearts.

What differentiates a great leader?

- The heart is where leadership really matters
- To be a great leader, to be successful and to finish well, you must develop the qualities of a great heart.
- One of the things that set one leader apart from the other is that Great Leaders lead from their hearts and guards diligently their hearts with the throne of their hearts dedicated to the fear of God.

For the throne mandate and assignment, God is looking for men and women whose hearts are after His own heart.

When Your Heart Is Set

Daniel 1:8, 9; 10:12
But Daniel purposed in his heart that he would not defile himself with the portion of the king's delicacies, nor with the wine which he drank; therefore he requested of the chief of the eunuchs that he might not defile himself. Now God had brought Daniel into the favor and goodwill of the chief of the eunuchs.
Do not fear, Daniel, for from the first day that you set your heart to understand and to humble yourself before your God, your words were heard; and I have come because of your words.

When your heart is set, God will dispatch dispensational angels to help you bring His purpose to pass and to influence the earth. When you come to the point of 'if I perish, I perish' concerning your mandate on the throne, heavenly resources are released to assist you. When your heart is set, the heavens give and release verdicts in your favour. Certain decisions are not taken in heaven until your heart is set in that direction. I believe strongly that one of the keys of the kingdom of heaven is the power of a heart that is set to do the will of God even at the cost of such life.

When Daniel made up his mind and purposed in his heart not to defile himself with the king's meat, heavens took the decision to influence the Chief of the Eunuchs to act according to the request of Daniel at the risk of his own head. Conversely, when your heart is not set, purposes are delayed, destroyed or perverted. And when your heart is set to walk in disobedience contrary to the principles and purpose of God for establishing the throne, you will have your way but, the consequences may bring problems to many generations. Be careful therefore what your heart is set to do and not to do. If you don't conclude certain matters and take a position in your heart to do what is right at all times, when trials, challenges of the throne and temptations come, you will be overtaken.

Psalm 57:7
My heart is fixed, O God, my heart is fixed: I will sing and give praise

It is pertinent to state that this cast of heart was integral to David's success on the throne and it is a timeless principle that will help any leader to succeed too. I don't know the current conditions of your heart, however if you want to prepare yourself to be used by God in any leadership position and be steadfast to the end, your heart is where to start. Take a decision with a strong determination to train yourself, fix and position your heart to choose good and reject evil, to love righteousness and to hate wickedness.

Recommended:
The Prayers of King David – Psalms 86:11-12; Psalms 119:36-38

- Teach me Your way, O LORD, I will walk in Your truth.
- Unite my heart to fear Your name.
- I will praise You, O Lord my God, with all my heart.
- I will glorify Your name forevermore.
- Incline my heart to Your testimonies, and not to covetousness.
- Turn away my eyes from looking at worthless things.
- Revive me in Your mercy.
- Establish Your word to Your servant, who is devoted to fearing You.

10.

INTEGRITY OF HEART

God is a God of Integrity – Numbers 23:19

God, the King of kings and Lord of lords, the creator of heavens and earth who created all the thrones is a God of integrity. It implies that creation and sustainability of creation are subject to the law and principles of integrity. The nature of integrity is that it holds all other attributes of good characters together. Remove integrity, creation is in disorder; take away integrity and relationships are destroyed. Compromise integrity and businesses are ruined, and nations are brought low.

We cannot afford not to commit ourselves to integrity and to raise men and women of integrity. Integrity will make you thrive anywhere in the world no matter the challenges. Integrity of heart and the skill of a leader will always tremendously affect the people and the prosperity of the land – this is both timeless and universal. It is one of the greatest virtues desired by most people in all spheres of human endeavours, be it friendship, marriage, business and government. It is a quality of high value needed both in private life between and as regards public responsibility.

When it comes to operating on the thrones, transforming our domain of influence and building legacy for generations to come, integrity of heart is priceless. It was with integrity of heart that King David operated on the throne and shepherded the nation of Israel. Integrity of heart is what God is searching for in the nation when it comes raising leaders to sit on the thrones to whom he gave a testimony and said, *'I have found David the son of Jesse, a man after My own heart, who will do all My will.'* (1 Samuel 13:14; Acts 13:22).

So, he shepherded them according to the integrity of his heart, and guided them by the skillfulness of his hands (Psalm 78:72)

Now if you walk before Me as your father David walked, in

integrity of heart and in uprightness, to do according to all that I have commanded you, and if you keep My statutes and My judgments, 5 then I will establish the throne of your kingdom over Israel forever, as I promised David your father, saying, 'You shall not fail to have a man on the throne of Israel.' 1 Kings 9:4

I know also, my God, that You test the heart and have pleasure in uprightness. As for me, in the uprightness of my heart I have willingly offered all these things; and now with joy I have seen Your people, who are present here to offer willingly to You. 1 Kings 9:5

Integrity is needed to operate as kings and leaders on the thrones and without this quality of the heart, the dynamics, assignments and the purpose of thrones will be compromised and truncated; which will affect the leader as well as the organization, community or nation. Integrity is a basic ingredient for the sustainable development of any organization, kingdom, community, and nation. Corruption and deceit which disintegrate any organization or nation, are the products of lack of integrity. Often, when people are taught about leadership they are not schooled in the basic principles of integrity. Even so, the number one area of personal transformation for sustainable leadership is rebuilding integrity. Integrity is beneficial across all spheres of life, including in our marriages and family life, in our business dealings, in politics and governance, and in everyday transactions.

The future of our families, communities and nations depends on our response today to the need to intentionally train and raise men and women with the right attitude, vision, mind-set, and integrity of heart to operate on the thrones. If a person possesses all the other attributes of a leader but lack integrity, whatever is built will be destroyed overtime. Prayers is very important, but prayer alone is not enough. We have to build integrity as a lifestyle in men and women because integrity is the foundation of our character and we need courage and wholesomeness of mind and spirit to establish the thrones and the land. It takes the voices of integrity in leadership to build nations and we are desperately in need of relevant and reliable wisdom, blueprints, and strategies from God on raising responsible leaders with integrity of heart.

What is Integrity?

Integrity is derived from a root word "integer" which means to be whole, complete or entire, as in a whole number. The Greeks word *'adiaphthoria'* translated 'integrity', means untaintedness and uprightness of character. It refers to authenticity, incorruptibility and sincerity. It is a demonstration of trustworthiness and purity of motive. Integrity is the quality of being honest and having strong moral discipline and principles. Integrity is about who we are and not what we appear to be. It is about having a strong sense of what is right or wrong and always holding on to doing what is right even at the point of death. It is also about admitting mistakes and doing what is necessary to put things right. The challenges of the thrones will reveal whether or not you have integrity.

The Nature and Underlying Principles of Integrity

I. Incorruptibility

Integrity means to be bluntly honest that you cannot be influenced by anything that is illegal or morally wrong. A good judge, for example, must be incorruptible, operating with ethical principles of fairness and equity. An incorruptible judge or leader cannot be bribed.

> *"**The king establishes (stabilizes) the land by justice, but a man who takes bribes overthrows it.**" Proverbs 29:4*

As a leader, you will always experience the temptation to put selfish goal or reward above the truth, fairness and equity but, you take a stand that it does not pay to give up your integrity for any reward whatever it maybe.

II. Wholeness of Life

Integrity means completeness and wholeness of life in that your way of life is in line with your behaviour. Recognizing the importance of integrity in leadership, Paul challenged and commanded Timothy, a young leader, not only to teach or preach the word but to set an example for the believers in speech, in life, in love, in faith and in purity – 1 Tim.4:11-12. To be whole is to be consistent in every area of life.

III. Adherence to Oath

Integrity means that you keep your promise or oath regardless of the cost. Joshua in his leadership was deceived into making a treaty with the Gibeonites, but once he made a covenant with them, he knew it was his duty to defend them Psa.15:4, Josh.10:15

IV. Uprightness of Character

Integrity means always behaving and acting honestly. *"In all things showing thyself a pattern of good works: in doctrine showing incorruptness, gravity, sincerity"* – Titus 2:7.

Character has become a crucial issue today because of many leaders in political, business and religious world who have fallen morally. A person's worth is not determined by his or her appearance, what really makes a person valuable lies below the surface – Integrity of heart. We judge by appearances when choosing leaders but, God's parameter is the heart. The nature of integrity is that it is an inner beauty that God seeks after. God cannot be confused by our big names and qualifications because He sees through our heart. He is looking for a heart of integrity, that man or woman after His own heart. We need training in character building and development to handle throne assignments.

V. Trustworthiness

Integrity involves building trust, being dependable, and the only way to build trust is to tell the truth even if it may disappoint. Integrity is a way of life committed to telling the truth which the opposite is of lying. Leadership can only function based on trust. Trust implies accountability, predictability, dependability, and reliability. It is indeed a tragedy for any leader to betray trust.

VI. Responsible Commitment

It is hard for most leaders to accept the responsibility for what happens in their organization. Often, leaders are tempted to reject taking responsibility for something bad or unpleasant. But leaders who take full responsibility for their own action and for the people over whom God has placed them will command loyalty and respect. Integrity means to be committed to taking full responsibility as a leader.

VII. State of Consistency

Integrity means the quality of the state of being consistent, the quality of always being the same not bowing to pressure but following through to the end. A way of life always committed to doing the right thing. God testified about the integrity of Job. Despite the loss of family, wealth, and health, the accusations of his friends, and the evil suggestion of his wife, Job maintained his integrity to the end. Job 2:1-10, 27:5-6.

VIII. Moral Uprightness

Integrity means a state of being of morally principled, upright in mind. The entire chapter of proverbs seven is a warning against immorality. The victim is a young man, an emerging leader who is naive and untaught in moral discipline. Since the father realizes that his son could yield to the same temptation, he admonishes his son to protect his heart or mind (v.25) before the time of temptation occurs. No Need of outside accountability: ***"How can I do such a wicked thing as this? It would be a great sin against God"*** (Gen. 39:8, 9).

This was the guiding light and principle in the heart of Joseph in Potiphar's house when his master's wife was asking her to have an affair with her, but he did not even though no one was supervising or watching him. No family member was there with Joseph, but his heart was established in integrity and the fear of God. Many leaders have been destroyed in this way and scheme. The nature of integrity is possessing an inner character of working faithfully, no need of outside accountability to keep doing what is right as the example of Joseph. Joseph viewed the sin of immorality with his master's wife as wickedness and not just a sin against his master but wickedness against God, the all-seeing.

Beware of immorality on the thrones
For the commandment is a lamp, and the law a light; reproofs of instruction are the way of life, to keep you from the evil woman, From the flattering tongue of a seductress. Do not lust after her beauty in your heart, nor let her allure you with her eyelids. For by means of a harlot a man is reduced to a crust of bread; and an adulteress will prey upon his precious life. Proverbs. 6:23-26

IX. Integrity Is a Guide – Prov.11:3

"

A good man is guided by his honesty, the evil man is destroyed by his dishonesty"

The nature of integrity is that it provides a guide to making good decisions in life especially when such decisions affect other lives, communities and nations.

X. A Lifetime Process

Integrity is not a one-time deal but a lifetime engagement and process. You must keep doing what is right. It is not a conditional or circumstantial thing. The person of integrity does not change because of pressure. It takes a lifetime to build integrity, but can be messed up in a day. "Integrity may make you to be unpopular or be the odd" man to start with but when you live a life of integrity, people will know and testify to it. Even, satan will testify to your integrity as it did about Job. The nature of Integrity is that what you believe is right is worth dying for (Esther 4:16). Standing for what is right in integrity demand total and absolute commitment even to the point of death. Did Esther perish? No.

Benefits of Integrity

Even though a lifestyle of integrity could be challenging, a lot of benefits abound for a person of integrity and the organization they lead. In fact, the blessings of integrity are transgenerational.

I. Integrity Advances God's Intervention – Proverbs 12:22

As we find in the examples of men and women who refused to bend the rules even at the point of death like Daniel, Esther, Job etc.

II. The Blessings of Integrity Are Transgenerational

*"**The just man walketh in his integrity: and his children are blessed after him**" – Prov. 20:7*

III. Integrity Preserves – Psalm 25: 21

IV. Integrity helps you to build personal self-esteem to help you combat battles of life – Hebrews 10:35-36

V. Integrity makes people trust you – 2 Corinthians 8:21

VI. It helps you to build a true and correct relationship – 1 Chronicles 29:17

VII. It helps you to have peace of mind – Psalm 25:21

VIII. It helps you to keep your focus and priority right in life – 2 Corinthians 8:21

IX. Integrity can keep you out of danger in life – Proverbs 28:18; 1 Peter 3:10.

X. It gives you the power and the strength you need to impact your domain positively – Proverbs 11

XI. Integrity will help you to empower and enhance your prayer life – 1 Chronicles 29:17

XII. Integrity will help you to make a difference in your community – 1 Kings 9:4-5

Practical Guide On Building a Lifestyle of Integrity

- Examine your heart prayerfully before God. "Search me, O God and know my heart try me, and know my thoughts, and see if there be any wicked way in me and lead me in the way everlasting". When you as a leader fail to deal with sin in your own life, the people who work with you will soon lose confidence in us.
- Do a personal check-up of your life and ask yourself practical questions. Am I truthful? Am I honest? Can God count on me as a person of integrity? Am I honest with myself and others? Can I be trusted? Am I dependable and trustworthy? Are you armed to justify yourself or are you willing to trust God and his word to help you overcome the deceitfulness of your own heart? There is no hiding place, the challenges and the temptations of the thrones will reveal who you are.
- Rediscover who you are and re-establish your identity in God, who is God of integrity and purpose in your heart like Daniel not to bow down to any other gods no matter your lot.
- Make a commitment to live a life of integrity: "But as for me, I will walk in mine integrity: redeem me, and be merciful unto me" – Psalm 26:11.
- Be ready to face the challenge and the price of integrity.
- Associate with men and women of integrity and distance yourself from men and women who lack integrity.
- Set rules and standards of integrity for your own life.

Commitment to a Lifestyle of Integrity

"But as for me, I will walk in mine integrity: redeem me, and be merciful unto me" (Psa. 26:11).

Make up your mind and be resolute to be a man or woman of integrity. Pray fervently until this change takes effect in every aspect of your life as a leader. If you must operate on the throne, you must muster every effort, determination and commit to live a life of integrity.

Prayer Cry for Integrity of Heart (Psalm 19:12-14)

"Who can understand his errors? Cleanse thou me from secret faults, keep back thy servant also from presumptuous sins. Let them not have dominion over me: then shall I be right, and I shall be innocent from the great transgression. Let the words of my mouth, and the meditation of my heart, be acceptable in thy sight, O Lord, my strength, and my redeemer"

11.

PREPARATION OF THE HEART FOR THE THRONE

Rehoboam: A King Who Did Not Prepare His Heart

King Rehoboam, the son of King Solomon was a disappointment. The strategic importance of his kingship in the history of ancient Israel is recorded in the Bible (1 Kings 12). It was during his tenure that the kingdom of ancient Israel was divided. When the people gathered in the city of Shechem for Rehoboam's coronation, the Israelites requested that he lighten the heavy workload his father, Solomon, previously imposed on the people. Rehoboam told the people to give him three days to consider their request.

During those three days, Rehoboam consulted two distinct groups of people. The first group comprised wise and experienced elders who served King Solomon during his reign (1 Kings 12:6). They understood what it took for a king to rule his people successfully. They told Rehoboam to heed the request of the people and lighten their workload. The elders knew this would cause Rehoboam to win the people's favour, and in turn, the people would welcome their new king's rule over them. However, Rehoboam rejected the elders' counsel (2 Kings 12:8). The second group Rehoboam consulted were his peers, friends Rehoboam grew up with who were inexperienced in life and ill-equipped to offer any valuable counsel for what he should do as king. King Rehoboam's friends gave foolish advice, as opposed to the counsel given by the wise elders.

They told Rehoboam to refuse the people's request and assert his authority over them by threatening worse labour conditions than those they experienced under Solomon (1Kings 12:10-11). Rehoboam foolishly heeded the advice of his friends. On the third day, when the people returned to hear the king's verdict, Rehoboam told them, "My father made your yoke heavy, but I will add to your yoke; my father disciplined you with whips, but I will discipline you with scorpions." (1 Kings 12:14).

In response to Rehoboam's foolish answer, the people rejected his rule and the Kingdom was divided, with two tribes subject to Rehoboam's rulership while the other ten tribes united under Jeroboam, the son of Nebat. It is critical to note that as much as that development in the history of ancient Israel was foretold in prophecy, Rehoboam's cast of mind was also a contributing factor. It is written concerning Rehoboam in 2 Chronicles 12:14, **"And he did evil, because he prepared not his heart to seek the LORD."**

Leadership is not Lordship; this is the importance of conditioning your heart to seek the Lord because effective leadership begins with the preparation of the heart to seek the LORD and do His will. If your heart is not prepared to seek the Lord it becomes the pattern of your life which will give room to wrong counsels. This is the difference between the good path and the evil path.

Proverb 16:1-3
The preparations of the heart belong to man, But the answer of the tongue is from the Lord.
All the ways of a man are pure in his own eyes, But the Lord weighs the spirits.
Commit your works to the Lord, And your thoughts will be established.
1 Samuel 7:3
And Samuel spoke unto all the house of Israel, saying, if you do return unto the LORD with all your hearts, then put away strange gods and Ashtaroth from among you and prepare your hearts unto the LORD, and serve him only.

The Word Prepare

The word prepare means to establish, fix, determine, purposed which implies a deliberate effort to do or not to do certain things. Daniel's resolve which took place at the beginning of his career no doubt set him up for a long, successful and illustrious decades as palace administrator. This is against Rehoboam who began his career with the opposite mind-set which brought disastrous outcome. It is written concerning Daniel: *"**But Daniel purposed in his heart that he would not defile himself with the portion of the king's meat, nor with the wine which he drank: therefore he requested of the prince of the***

eunuchs that he might not defile himself." Daniel 1:8 (KJV). The word fixed or purposed is to set firmly in position, not subject to change or variation and firmly held in the mind.

Psalm 57:7
"My heart is fixed, O God, my heart is fixed: I will sing and give praise."
Daniel 10:12
"Do not fear, Daniel, for from the first day that you set your heart to understand, and to humble yourself before your God, your words were heard, and I have come because of your words.

Let your heart be fixed on what you will do and will not do before you encounter the temptations and challenges of the thrones for you will encounter many daunting challenges on the thrones. What Joseph did when Potiphar's wife tried to tempt him to sin demonstrate that Joseph's heart was already set and fixed not to yield to sexual perversion. He understood it as great wickedness not even against Potiphar but, against God. **Joseph's mind-set was that he cannot do wickedness against God no matter what it will cost him – Genesis 39:7-9**. To this extent, Joseph has made up his mind and purposed in his heart not to yield to temptation that confronts him daily while doing his business. This certainly is part of God's preparation for Joseph for the throne later as Prime Minister of Egypt.

Genesis 39:7-9
And it came to pass after these things that his master's wife cast longing eyes on Joseph, and she said, "Lie with me." But he refused and said to his master's wife, "Look, my master does not know what is with me in the house, and he has committed all that he has to my hand. There is no greater in this house than I, nor has he kept back anything from me but you, because you are his wife. How then can I do this great wickedness, and sin against God?"

The word of God says we should guard our heart with all diligence because out it flows the issues of life (Proverbs 4:23). This means whatever we allow to enter our hearts, if not examined and properly evaluated, will in the end form our habit and be expressed in our lives and actions – in positive or negative ways. What Daniel and Joseph did is definition of diligently guarding the heart which will definitely enhance your reign on the throne or your leadership position in your domain of influence. Another aspect of the preparation of the heart is through prayer, study of the word and living by the truth of the word.

- **Discover the truth, do it and teach the truth – Ezra 7:10**

For Ezra had prepared his heart to seek the Law of the LORD, to do it, and to teach statutes and ordinances in Israel. This verse reflects the priority and the heart of Ezra, the priest; a leader fully committed to his God and leading the people right. You cannot give what you don't have. Ezra's model is a lesson for those in leadership position: study and discover the truth, live by the truth and the principles, teach, train and commit it to other men as well.

- **Pray over and commit your heart daily to God – Psalm 19:14**

Let the words of my mouth and the meditation of my heart be acceptable in Your sight, O LORD, my strength and my Redeemer.

Strategic Principles for the Preparation of the Heart
With the inherent conditions of the heart and its significance to life and leadership, there is a need to carefully prepare our hearts for it is the Throne of God.

- **Preparation Through Repentance** – 1 Samuel 7:3; Jeremiah 24:7; Psalm 51

1 Samuel 7:3
And Samuel spake unto all the house of Israel, saying, If ye do return unto the Lord with all your hearts, then put away the strange gods and Ashtaroth from among you, and prepare your hearts unto the Lord, and serve him only: and he will deliver you out of the hand of the Philistines.

The preparation of your heart can be hindered without a proper repentance and deception. You really need to confess every sin that you can remember so that God's rain of righteousness can come upon you (Hosea 10:12). You need to renounce every wicked ways and ask that your heart be established in the fear of God. The fear of God is the beginning of wisdom (Proverbs 1:7; 9:10-12). Since all wars and fighting come from the corruptions of our own hearts, it is right to mortify those lusts that war in the members through genuine repentance.

Invite God to Prepare your Heart – Psalm 10:17
No one can accomplish preparing their heart on their own.

Psalm 10:7
*"LORD, thou hast heard the desire of the humble; **thou wilt prepare their heart.**"*

You need to recognize the conditions of your heart, acknowledge your need for help and deliberately and sincerely cry to God to prepare your heart to do His will on the throne. You need to develop an attitude whereby in humility you sincerely and willingly invite God to examine the conditions of your heart daily when you are a king or you occupy a significant position of leadership.

Psalm 139:23, 24
Search me, O God, and know my heart: try me, and know my thoughts: and see if there be any wicked way in me and lead me in the way everlasting.

God's intervention is dependent on a humble and submissive heart. Humility is a priceless asset when it comes to the preparation of the heart for the thrones. When a person begins to fall, is either such person has forsaken or neglected the art of humility and his or her heart is lifted up in pride. The humility of the heart is a great virtue and an important character of a successful leader. We know that God resists the proud and gives grace to the humble (1Pet.5:5) and also He leads the humble in what is right, and teaches the humble His way (Psa. 25:9).

Humility is the opposite of pride, characterised by the following attributes that were used to describe the humility of Christ Jesus in Philippians 2:8:

- It is an attitude – a state of the mind, inward and genuine willingness not to allow your position to enter your head.
- It is characterised by a deliberate act of emptying yourself – no reputation
- It manifests in total obedience to God's commandment even unto death.

Proverb 16:18

"Pride goeth before destruction, and a haughty spirit before a fall."

Going by what is clearly written above, we need to take a deliberate step or action to humble ourselves.

- **Preparation Through the Power of Memorial – Psalm 78:1-11**

One great error that people easily fall into is to forget the faithfulness and the mighty works that God has performed in the past that they quickly turn back from God and behave as if through their own power they are on the throne. God told the children of Israel to tell each succeeding generation the testimony of His faithfulness so that they may set their hope in God and may not become a stubborn and rebellious generation that do not set its heart aright (Psalm 78:8). The intent and imaginations of our heart plays an important role in the preparation of our hearts. In his praises to God for the offerings to build the temple of God, whose temple we are; King David prayed that God will use the memory of the event to prepare the hearts of the people.

1 Chronicles 29:16-19.
David prayed "O LORD our God, all this abundance that we have prepared to build You a house for Your holy name is from Your hand and is all Your own. I know also, my God, that You test the heart and have pleasure in uprightness. As for me, in the uprightness of my heart I have willingly offered all these things; and now with joy I have seen Your people, who are present here to offer willingly to You. O LORD God of Abraham, Isaac, and Israel, our fathers, keep

this forever in the intent of the thoughts of the heart of Your people, and fix their heart toward You. And give my Solomon a loyal heart...

When your heart is dominated with thoughts of His faithfulness and goodness, it is difficult for you to turn back from the LORD. The children of Israel, the generation that left Egypt forgot the works of God and they perished in the Wilderness except Caleb and Joshua. There is power in declaring daily the eternal faithfulness of God. It is a strategy to keep our hearts glued to Him, to overcome temptation and falling away.

Components of the prepared heart.

- **Modesty and Frugality: Refusing to Abuse Power and Authority**

Nehemiah the builder is a practical example of leading transformation with modesty and frugality. Nehemiah having served in the Persian court as a cupbearer must have been used to the lavish food and luxury there. Yet, knowing the relatively modest means of a territory that was being rebuilt, Nehemiah contented himself with even less than the governors who ruled before him. He even restrained his aides from pressuring the people.

Nehemiah 5:14-18
Moreover from the time that I was appointed to be their governor in the land of Judah, from the twentieth year even unto the two and thirtieth year of Artaxerxes the king, that is, twelve years, I and my brethren have not eaten the bread of the governor.
But the former governors that had been before me were chargeable unto the people, and had taken of them bread and wine, beside forty shekels of silver; yea, even their servants bare rule over the people: but so did not I, because of the fear of God.
Yea, also I continued in the work of this wall, neither bought we any land: and all my servants were gathered thither unto the work. Moreover there were at my table an hundred and fifty of the Jews and rulers, beside those that came unto us from among the heathen that are about us.

The main lesson here is that Nehemiah prepared his heart not to be a burden to his people, not to exploit the people and not to abuse his power and position. Beyond that, for twelve years Nehemiah did not receive salary. Nehemiah's example is a reminder that kings and leaders must be modest, act ethically, responsibly and be resolute not to abuse their powers and positions.

- **The Heart of a Shepherd** – Psalm 78:72

King David Shepherded Israel according to the integrity of his heart, he guided them by the skilfulness of his hands. Shepherd –is the most prominent metaphor for Leadership and Psalm 23 teaches us the ways in which God, The Great Shepherd leads His people. In John 10, Jesus also referred to Himself as the Good Shepherd and the attributes of a good shepherd. The prophet Ezekiel wrote a great prophecy and warnings from the LORD against 'shepherds of Israel who have not led or cared for God's people well'- Ezekiel 34:1-10

- **An Understanding Heart**

Leadership, governance and operating on the thrones is a serious affair. You are responsible for the lives of other people. Your decisions will affect people sometime even beyond the borders of your nation or kingdom. Wisdom or lack of it will bring prosperity or ruin to the nation. A heart that can discern what is good from evil is an understanding heart. Wisdom is the extraordinary principle and skill in management

1 King 3:8, 9
"And Your servant is in the midst of Your people whom You have chosen, a great people, too numerous to be numbered or counted. Therefore give to Your servant an understanding heart to judge Your people, that I may discern between good and evil. For who is able to judge this great people of Yours?"

- **Largeness of Heart – 1 King 4:29**

Largeness of heart is another type of a great leader's heart. Largeness of heart helps to solve many problems. A narrow or small heart manifests foolishness. Pride is a manifestation of foolishness and a product of narrow mindedness; inability to see the bigger picture of the purpose of the throne. The root of incompetence comes from a narrow heart. Leaders need much wisdom and largeness of heart.

1 Kings 4:29

And God gave Solomon wisdom and understanding exceeding much, and largeness of heart, even as the sand that is on the seashore.

- **A Honest Heart**

Psalm 51:6 TLB

You deserve honesty from the heart; yes, utter sincerity and truthfulness. Oh, give me this wisdom

Honesty in the heart: Truthfulness, Genuineness and Sincerity. Being honest with ourselves, others, and God requires admitting we're imperfect. Doing so is humbling, but the rewards are worth it. Honesty opens the door for forgiveness, reconciliation, and restoration when we are honest enough to admit our mistakes and limitation. Honesty paves the way for us to grow in wisdom and learn from our mistakes.

"As I have said, the first thing is to be honest with yourself. You can never have an impact on society if you have not changed yourself."-
Nelson Mandela

- **An Obedient Heart**

The first king to be anointed in the Bible was removed for the sin of disobedience. He feared the people more than God who raised him up to be king over His people. When God raise you to any position of authority, you must remember your first allegiance must be to Him to walk in obedience.

1 Samuel 15:22, 23
And Samuel said, Hath the Lord as great delight in burnt offerings and sacrifices, as in obeying the voice of the Lord? Behold, to obey is better than sacrifice, and to hearken than the fat of rams.
For rebellion is as the sin of witchcraft, and stubbornness is as iniquity and idolatry. Because thou hast rejected the word of the Lord, he hath also rejected thee from being king.

Obedience is better than sacrifice is a golden rule: better to obey God than a man. Obedience must be complete, nothing like partial obedience – God removed King Saul for disobedience. There is a need to deal with stubbornness, rebellion in the heart and pray for a heart of obedience

- **A Loyal Heart**

For the eyes of the Lord run to and fro throughout the whole earth, to show Himself strong on behalf of those whose heart is loyal to Him – 2 Chronicles 16:9. Pretension or hypocrisy does not work with God, nothing can be hidden from Him. No detail is too little or too distant; He sees not only our actions but also our very motives, intentions, and thoughts. God sees the real you always, what others do not see or know about you is naked before God. In Hebrew, the word loyal is translated "salem" which means complete and perfect. There is something amazing about King Amaziah:

2 Chronicles 25:2
And he did that which was right in the sight of the Lord, but not with a perfect heart.

Despite all of the good things about King Amaziah's life, there was something missing, something not right in his heart and not his actions! Did he love God? Most certainly he did. Did he serve God? Yes, he did. Did he do right and good things? Yes! But, did he love Him and serve Him with all of his heart? No...he did not. When you know that a security camera is watching you, you tend to be more conscious of your actions because you know you are being monitored. What if we keep it constantly in our hearts that God's all seeing eyes is watching us, how will that change our attitude and actions?

- **A Heart of Compassion**

When you set aside your indifference and connect with those who are in pain. A feeling of deep sympathy and sorrow for another who is stricken by misfortune, accompanied by a strong desire to alleviate the suffering. When you are moved in your heart by the conditions of the poor and the needy. Leaders must allow the Holy Spirit to change their hearts from a heart of indifference and cruelty to a heart of compassion. A compassionate heart comes with grace and actions to bring a positive change like Nehemiah.

- **A Servant Heart – Luke 22:24 -30**

What really is a servant heart? A true servant heart is made up of who you are and how you feel – a combination of good character and attitude that lend you to serve the needs of others with humility, compassion, courage and a sense of responsibility. Being a servant leader means shouldering leadership responsibilities by making people's growth and development a priority not using position of power, authority or influence as the only tools for leading. To operate on the thrones and succeed is never based on charisma or eloquence of speech, but courage to empty yourself and take the form of a servant, speak good words to your people and answer them properly.

1 Kings 12:7
And they spake unto him, saying, If thou wilt be a servant unto this people this day, and wilt serve them, and answer them, and speak good words to them, then they will be thy servants forever.

· **A Detribalized Heart**

Tribalism is entrenched everywhere in the nations, workplaces and marketplaces. Nations need visionary and detribalised leadership to fulfil their corporate destiny Detribalization takes place in the heart and is very crucial, because what destroys a nation most often are inter-tribal issues and conflicts that are deeply rooted in the hearts. By a detribalized heart, I mean a heart that is devoid of hatred and prejudice against other people or tribes having being healed of what other tribes have done to your tribe and willing to embrace others and trusting them that together you can build a healthy and sustainable atmosphere and society. For this purpose, Christ has redeemed us out of every tribe, people and tongue as a kingdom of priests to serve our God and to bear of rulership that is devoid of tribalism and hatred (Revelation 5:9,10).

A CASE FOR SOUTH AFRICA: DEVELOPING A RAINBOW HEART FOR A RAINBOW NATION

Archbishop Desmond Tutu coined the concept of the Rainbow Nation to describe post-apartheid South Africa, after the first democratic, multiracial election of 1994.

The following quote is credited to him:

And you remember the rainbow in the Bible is the sign of peace. The rainbow is the sign of prosperity. We want peace, prosperity and justice and we can have it when all the people of God, the rainbow people of God, work together – **Desmond Tutu**

To get a wind of God's purpose and burden for nation building, we need to examine the burdens, intents, cries, yearning desires, deliberations and visions of the nation's founding fathers in their struggle for independence. You need to examine the historical documents like the declaration of independence, national anthem, pledge, Bill of Right etc.., More importantly Desmond Tutu also stated:

"There will be no future without forgiveness. Any process of peace is bound to collapse if this is missing. There is no way peace and stability can come through the gun of vengeance" **Desmond Tutu**

The phrase was later elaborated by President Nelson Mandela:

"We have triumphed in the effort to implant hope in the breasts of the millions of our people. We enter into a covenant that we shall build the society in which all South Africans, both black and white, will be able to walk tall, without any fear in their hearts, assured of their inalienable right to human dignity – a rainbow nation at peace with itself and the world" – **Nelson Mandela.**

Nelson Mandela (Madiba) however made this statement about himself which I believe is a critical point in achieving a true rainbow nation:

"As I walked out the door toward the gate that would lead to my freedom, I knew if I didn't leave my bitterness and hatred behind, I'd still be in prison." – **Nelson Mandela**

Truth and Reconciliation Commission (TRC) was set up after the government of Mandela was inaugurated to address the injustices of past apartheid regime. The TRC tried their best, but the nation needed a deeper dimension of healing. Ironically majority of the racial and cultural groups of the people are still in prison. Someone even wrote that the rainbow nation of Nelson Mandela and Desmond Tutu is dead. There is nothing that destroys a nation more than inter-tribal, racial conflicts and unhealed issues in the nation's history. In our work in South Africa, I see that the people are yet to heal totally and that the hatred locked up in the hearts of racial groupings are very deep and hard to be broken.

Yet I strongly believe in Rainbow mandate of the nation, however we need to face the brutal facts in the spirit of genuine repentance, forgiveness, reconciliation, and unity for the nation to fulfil her corporate destiny where each tribe will be able to contribute to the corporate identity and the skills of the nation for sustainable development.

For this purpose, I make a case for **The Rainbow Heart Initiative** and call on the nation to take the bull by the horn and begin to address the monster of racial hatred from city to city and province to province starting with each individual like Nelson Mandela did. This a spiritual project and process for healing and reconciliation that must be handled with due diligence. Let the healing begin with you. For the nation to truly attain her prophetic identity and significant status of a Rainbow Nation at peace with itself and the world, in order to fulfil her corporate destiny, we need Rainbow Hearts for the Rainbow nation. This will involve a pragmatic training, interventions, and initiatives for the attainment of detribalized hearts to really become The Rainbow People of God. This is an extremely huge task.

PREPARE YOUR HEART IN ADVANCE

- Daniel purposed in his heart that he would not defile himself with the portion of the king's delicacies in advance…. Daniel 1:8
- The way to subdue your impulses is by activating your will – in advance.
- When you activate your will, God empowers you by His Spirit.
- Develop a strong sense of purpose by activating your will in advance to do righteousness and justice.
- You will set yourself up for failure if you fail to develop a strong sense of purpose in advance.
- The battle between the flesh and the spirit is a daily battle.
- This battle is intensified when you are on the throne or any leadership position.
- You need to prepare in advance before the temptations of the thrones come.
- You cannot wish or pray temptations away, but you can prepare yourself in advance to overcome temptations, evil and wickedness on the throne.
- This is apart from the challenges of taking hard decisions, leading and proffering solutions on the throne. You may need to call in reinforcements when you need help.

Take the Oath of Integrity and Promised Faithfulness on the Throne
Psalm 101: The Oath of Office

I will sing of mercy and judgment: unto thee, O Lord, will I sing.

I will behave myself wisely in a perfect way. O when wilt thou come unto me?

I will walk within my house with a perfect heart.

I will set no wicked thing before mine eyes: I hate the work of them that turn aside; it shall not cleave to me.

A froward heart shall depart from me: I will not know a wicked person.

Whoso privily slandereth his neighbour, him will I cut off: him that hath an high look and a proud heart will not I suffer.

Mine eyes shall be upon the faithful of the land, that they may dwell with me: he that walketh in a perfect way, he shall serve me.

He that worketh deceit shall not dwell within my house: he that telleth lies shall not tarry in my sight.

I will early destroy all the wicked of the land; that I may cut off all wicked doers from the city of the Lord.

12.

TAKE AWAY THE WICKED FROM BEFORE THE KING

Take Away the Wicked

Take away the wicked is a command every king or leader must obey and not a suggestion in order to have stable and successful reign. The rule is that evil and wicked official must be removed before the throne of even a good ruler can be established and the kingdom and nation can prosper in righteousness. The inspired wisdom emphatically stated the key to good governance and the need to eliminate corrupt and wicked people and influences from before the king. Direct implication is that in the matter of kings, thrones and good governance we must see beyond kings alone; we need to also focus on training officials and the king's chamberlains to do righteousness and justice as well. King David in his promised faithfulness to God on the throne made an integrity vow to remove wicked and evil people from his company and from the land (Psalm 101).

Psalm 101: The Oath of Office By King David

"...I will set no wicked thing before mine eyes: I hate the work of them that turn aside; it shall not cleave to me.

A froward heart shall depart from me: I will not know a wicked person.

Whoso privily slandereth his neighbour, him will I cut off: him that hath an high look and a proud heart will not I suffer.

Mine eyes shall be upon the faithful of the land, that they may dwell with me: he that walketh in a perfect way, he shall serve me.

He that worketh deceit shall not dwell within my house: he that telleth lies shall not tarry in my sight.

I will early destroy all the wicked of the land; that I may cut off all wicked doers from the city of the Lord.

Before he died, he also gave instructions to Solomon to take away Joab, who had served as his army general throughout his reign for shedding innocent blood and one other evil man, Shimei (1 king 2:5-10). In a wave of national revival, another king Asa banished the perverted persons from the land and dethroned his grandmother from the exalted position of queen mother because of her wickedness.

"Also he removed Maachah his grandmother from being queen mother, because she had made an obscene image of Asherah. ..." 1 *Kings 15:13*

In the above scenario, the family dynamics is implicated. Family dynamics can impact the reign of a king or a leader either positively or negatively. Negative family dynamics such as the idolatry in the exalted position of a queen mother to King Asa could easily bring down his reign, but King Asa took courage to depose her from the exalted position and destroyed her idols.

"Take away the dross from the silver, and the smith has material for a vessel; take away the wicked from the presence of the king and his throne will be established in righteousness." Prov. 25:4, 5

The Bible is no doubt a political and good governance manual: a deliberate action must be taken to remove the wicked from before kings and leaders. Sometimes, good kings fail not because they want to fail, but because they lack the discernment and the courage to remove wicked people around them. King David and later King Solomon understood this dynamic by first-hand experience. David had to manage Joab before Solomon eliminated him.

Joab was David's nephew and Solomon's uncle. This is another indication that sometimes removing the wicked from before the king can run into a family dynamic.

A Good Ruler is Silver, and Wicked Advisors are the Dross

The context adds further weight to this proverb (Proverb 25:4). A good ruler is silver, and wicked advisors are the dross. If the dross is taken away, the purified ruler will be able to lead his kingdom to wonderful prosperity. Righteousness exalts a nation; therefore wickedness must be publicly crushed to obtain God's blessing (Proverb 14:34; 20:26). Dross is a good term for the scum that gathers in high places to siphon a living from legitimate rulers. But a great leader will drive them away as with a refiner's fire (Proverb 20:8).

Who Are The People Described As Wicked?
The Psalmist describes the character of the wicked in Psalm 10:2-11.

"The wicked in his pride persecutes the poor; Let them be caught in the plots which they have devised. For the wicked boasts of his heart's desire; He blesses the greedy and renounces the LORD. The wicked in his proud countenance does not seek God; God is in none of his thoughts. His ways are always prospering; Your judgments are far above, out of his sight; As for all his enemies, he sneers at them. He has said in his heart, "I shall not be moved; I shall never be in adversity. His mouth is full of cursing and deceit and oppression; under his tongue is trouble and iniquity. He sits in the lurking places of the villages; in the secret places he murders the innocent; His eyes are secretly fixed on the helpless. He lies in wait secretly, as a lion in his den; He lies in wait to catch the poor; He catches the poor when he draws him into his net. So he crouches, he lies low, that the helpless may fall by his strength. He has said in his heart, "God has forgotten; He hides His face; He will never see."

- They are morally corrupt, arrogant, aggressive and unjust oppressors.
- Their pride and violence spell disaster for any throne where they are allowed to operate.
- They influence kings (all authority) to subvert justice and do wickedness.
- They persecute the poor
- They bless the greedy and renounces the Lord
- They are full of deceit, cursing, oppression and iniquity
- God is never in their thoughts

Why the Wicked Must Be Removed from Before the King

Wise rulers have counsellors to assist in decisions and implement decisions. They cannot know all the details of every part of the kingdom or nation, so they rely on counsellors for help. But if these advisors are wicked, a good ruler will be corrupted by evil influence and deceit. These evil men must be removed, so the kingdom or nation can prosper in righteousness. Proximity to power has potential to and does amplify evil.

Proximity to the throne gives the wicked privileged access to deceive kings and use his influence to foment evil. Haman, the son of Hammedatha the Agagite is a good example of this. Haman was an ungodly wicked person who was promoted by King Ahasuerus above all the princes who were with him. Haman conspired to destroy all the Jews who were in Shushan because Mordecai, the Jew refused to make obeisance to him. The conspiracy of Haman and how he was destroyed are recorded in the book of Esther.

Interaction Between Good and Bad Counsels

The Rehoboam saga is an excellent example of how bad and wicked counsellors can swindle and overthrow good counsel. Competition between good and bad counsel is a poor and dangerous strategy. Rehoboam followed his father, Solomon, as king of Israel. Because Solomon had heavily taxed the nation, the people offered to serve Rehoboam forever, if he would ease their burden a little. Instead of listening to the wise advice of his father's counsellors and reducing taxes, he followed the advice of his young friends and harshly threatened the nation with higher taxes. Ten tribes revolted and left Rehoboam only the tribes of Judah and Benjamin (I Kings 12:1-19). Rehoboam never ruled his father's expansive nation a single day, for wicked counsellors, his boyhood friends, cost him most of the nation.

Evil Communications Corrupt Good Manners

The lesson is simple. Paul taught it as well. ***"Be not deceived: evil communications corrupt good manners"*** (I Corinthians 15:33). False information and wicked influence destroy truth and justice. Men of evil character must be avoided like a plaque and removed. The consequences of breaking this rule are much greater for a king and leaders than just a single citizen.

A whole nation can suffer greatly if wicked men corrupt a ruler with sinful or criminal advice and deceit. Nations today are cursed with a legion of men and women who are shady individuals, and yet high rulers are often subject to their subtle and dangerous influence. They include lobbyists, news analysts, public relations specialists, speechwriters, pollsters, interns, special interest groups, party donors, aides, and other sycophants who prey on the legitimate work of qualified men. We must pray for God to deliver elected and appointed rulers and administrators from such advisors or influence (I Timothy 2:1-2).

Haman, A Wicked Counsellor

A whole chapter of the Bible is written to describe the wicked intrigue of Haman, a wicked counsellor who had the ear of King Ahasuerus of the Persian Empire. Haman hated the Jews, because of Mordecai's lack of public worship, he slandered them to the king and enticed the King to authorize their extermination. It was only by the intervention of Esther the queen that she, Mordecai, and the rest of her people were saved.

Herodias, Wicked Power Behind the Throne

Herod Antipas, son of Herod the Great, was tetrarch of Galilee from 4 BC – AD 39. He married his brother Philip's wife, Herodias, for which John the Baptist rebuked him. Herod feared John, knew he was just and holy, and heard him gladly. But Herodias used a subtle ploy to trap Herod into beheading him against his will, for she hated John for his criticism of her adultery (Mark 6:17-29).

Be Wise, Keep Away Wicked Men and Women from Your Throne

Every man must keep his rule as husband, father, employer, or pastor pure from corruption. The only perfect counsel for these offices is found in the Word of God, which is superior to the opinions of all men and able to make the man of God perfect. There is one King about whom you need not worry. There are no evil advisors in His presence. The wicked shall not stand in His sight – He hates all workers of iniquity (Psalm 5:5). No one without perfectly sanctified character shall ever enter His kingdom (Rev 21:27). God has ordained His throne forever, and of the increase of his government there shall be no end and that is the throne of Jesus Christ. As a king or a leader, you need to invite the Lordship of Jesus Christ over your throne every day.

Importance of Wise and Faithful Counsellors

Wise and faithful counsellors are crucial for successful government. The longevity of a ruler is dependent on righteousness (Proverb 16:12; 29:14). The grave concern facing every leader is to find wise and faithful counsellors. King David rejected evil men from his service and company (Psalm 101:3-8; 119:63). David also gave deathbed instructions for Solomon to kill two officials, even though one was David's nephew and had served as general of the army his entire reign (I Kings 2:5-10).

Characteristics of Wise Counsellors

Jethro told Moses, "***Thou shalt provide out of all the people able men, such as fear God, men of truth, hating covetousness; and place such over them***" (Exodus 18:21).

- Able men
- Such as fear God
- Men of truth
- Hating Covetousness

And King Jehoshaphat charged the judges in his day, "***Take heed what ye do: for ye judge not for man, but for the LORD, who is with you in the judgment. Wherefore now let the fear of the LORD be upon you; take heed and do it: for there is no iniquity with the LORD our God, nor respect of persons, nor taking of gifts***" (II Chronicles 19:6-7).

Joseph, the Prime Minister of Egypt

But there are examples of the opposite sort. When Pharaoh needed a man to oversee the largest food storage and distribution plan in world history, where embezzlement and fraud could have been rife, he chose Joseph. He said to his servants regarding him, "Can we find such a one as this is, a man in whom the Spirit of God is?" And he made him the highest ruler in Egypt because "there is none so discreet and wise as thou art."

Daniel, the Palace Administrator

Daniel, a Jewish captive, served Nebuchadnezzar, Belshazzar, Darius the Mede, Cyrus the Persian, and other kings over a period of seventy-five years. As it was often customary to kill previous counsellors for concerns of loyalty when an empire changed hands, this tenure is phenomenal. How and why did it occur?

Daniel was a glorious and righteous counsellor by faithfulness and God's great blessings (Daniel 1:19-21; 2:48-49; 5:11; 6:25-28). When Daniel was intensely scrutinized and investigated by jealous peers, "they could find none occasion nor fault; forasmuch as he was faithful, neither was there any error or fault found in him" (Daniel 6:4). The issue about good governance is still: ***"Can we find such a one as this, a man in whom the Spirit of God is?"*** – Genesis 41:38

13.

THE THRONE IS ESTABLISHED BY RIGHTEOUSNESS

Righteousness and Justice: The Inspired Rules for Ideal Government
God ordained government authority over nations, and He laid the foundations and gave the rules for ideal government on the earth.

> *"You shall appoint for yourself judges and officers in all your towns which the Lord your God is giving you, according to your tribes, and they shall judge the people with righteous judgment."*
> Deuteronomy 16:18
> *"And in mercy shall a throne be established: and he shall sit in truth in the tabernacle of David, judging, and seeking judgment, and hasting righteousness".* Isaiah 16:5

Clearly stated, authority and leadership should be initiated and maintained by righteousness and justice. Kings and leaders must love and embrace righteousness, but hate wickedness (Psalm 45:7, Proverbs 16:10, 12, 13). The fortune of the king or the leader and the people depend on whether they work with these fundamental rules or not. A king, or any ruler, must be righteous to be worthy of his office and able to discharge his duties rightly. The people in any organisation or a nation will submit to and support a leader that earns their respect by righteousness and justice. But they will eventually reject a wicked king or leader. God will bless a righteous king or leader with wisdom and protection, but He will overthrow a wicked king or leader.

Therefore, God has set righteousness and justice as the ideal standard and foundation for the throne and for great government (Proverbs 20:28; 29:4,14). A faithful and noble king or leader, acting justly and wisely for the interests of his people, his throne, or his office and its authority, will be secured and territory will be blessed. This standard principle applies to all authority – parents, employers, kings (monarchs) and all those in authority. The functioning of the concept of righteousness is to be taught and worked out in the different spheres of human endeavour. Righteousness and justice must be the establishment of an organised society in all spheres of existence.

A king or leader will secure the functional authority of his office as long as he does what is right and administer justice. For this purpose, leaders should humble themselves before this inspired rule, for the effectiveness and length of authority and influence depend on how you demonstrate hatred for wickedness and uphold righteousness and justice.

The Concept of Righteousness

As stated above, righteousness and justice is a timeless concept. It is a critical and fundamental theme of thrones and good governance. The theme runs throughout the Bible, but many people misunderstand what they mean. The Hebrew word for "righteousness" is **tzedek,** and it means "rightness." It refers to something or someone that operates rightly and in alignment with the standards for which it is designed. It is acting in alignment with what is "right." Righteousness is standing for and doing what is right, it is a way of life that is all about doing what is right even when it is costly to do so. It is characterised by self-restraint, truthfulness, and straightforwardness. Doing an unpopular thing that is ethical requires righteousness.

The Concept of Justice

Justice is the Hebrew word **mishpat**, and it refers to the wise and consistent application of standards. The concept is usually associated with judgements or decisions that set things right while righteousness describes personal involvement in dealing with injustices and standing for what is ethical. This is a constant concern in every domain of influence, because the way of solving the problem of destructions in any organisation and the society is by applying the principles of justice in all aspects of governance.

Why Righteousness and Justice is Important

· **God Delights in Righteousness and Justice**

Jeremiah tells us that God actually delights in righteousness and justice: "Thus says the Lord: "*Let not the wise man boast in his wisdom, let not the mighty man boast in his might, let not the rich man boast in his riches, but let him who boasts boast in this, that he understands and knows me, that I am the Lord who practices steadfast love, justice, and righteousness in the earth. For in these things I delight, declares the Lord.*" (Jeremiah 9.23-24). Again, it is written: "*To do righteousness and justice is more acceptable to the Lord than sacrifice*." Proverbs 21:3

· **When the Righteous are in Authority, People Rejoice**

"*When the righteous are in authority, the people rejoice, But when a wicked man rules, people groan*" (Proverbs 29:2). It is the cornerstone of the social system. It is the basis for the coherent living of a society. Where there is injustice, there abounds chaos and all manners of unrest. In 1963, Dr. Martin Luther King said: "Injustice anywhere is a threat to justice everywhere. We are caught in an inescapable network of mutuality, tied in a single garment of destiny. Whatever affects one directly, affects all indirectly."

· **Righteousness exalts a nation**

The presence and practice of righteousness makes an organization or a nation strong, but wickedness degrades an organization and weakens it. The government must be founded on God's righteousness to have true justice in a nation. "*Righteousness exalts a nation, but evil is a reproach to any people*" (Proverbs 14:34). God's righteousness should be our measurement, not our own thoughts or beliefs. God expect the earthly thrones to be established and operated on these pillars and foundations of righteousness and justice. Sin refers to any deviation from what is right, or the failure to exercise justice. If a nation rejects objective standards, and/or it fails to consistently apply the standards, that nation becomes a society at risk.

The Challenge

God has ordained righteousness and justice as the pillars of a healthy society. This is the way He has designed the people, the leaders and the nations to operate. The aim is that righteousness and justice must be applied in the private, public, and political spheres. This reality presents a strategic challenge, because for a nation to prosper, it must be built on the foundation of right standards, and the wise and consistent application of the standards. Any deviation from this ideal standard, chaos and decay in society is inevitable. Righteousness and justice must become the responsibility of the citizens and the leaders of an organisation, a community and a nation. Unfortunately, the world at large today cares little for righteousness and justice. We live in serious times, and we face significant challenges of bad leadership and governance among the nations.

Moreover, the Christian community seems to lack the skill to take bold initiatives to teach righteousness and justice to the world that is becoming increasingly complex. The creator established the application of the principles of justice and righteousness as the solution to chaos and socio-economic disorder in any given sphere, but the same principle is being compromised through humanistic ideologies breeding a wicked society. Today, people engage with power to corrupt themselves, their organisations and society.

Developing The Character of Righteousness and Justice

Proverbs 16:10 -13 gives a challenge to anyone in position of authority. It teaches that righteousness is what establishes authority. While a multitude of theories and books offer differing views on how to be an effective leader, the Bible offers the concept of righteousness. Authority and righteousness must go together. Kings and all in position of authority must possess virtuous character to preserve their authority and office.

"In righteousness you will be established; you will be far from oppression, for you will not fear; and from terror, for it will not come near you". Isaiah 54:14

Your talent may lift you up before others, but your lack of character will bring you down if you compromise standing for what is right. Abraham Lincoln said, 'Nearly all men can stand adversity, but if you want to test a man's character, give him power.' You will face many challenges and temptations once you ascend the throne or when you are lifted up to any leadership position. In the hour of temptation, you will be called upon to choose one of two paths: character or compromise. And every time you choose character, you become stronger, even when your choice comes at a cost. It's easier to focus on our talent because, generally speaking, it produces results that are rewarded and celebrated by others, but if you desire better leadership success, character development is sacrosanct and character is built in private. It is written: *"The king gives stability to the land by justice, but a man who takes bribes overthrows it"*. Proverbs 29:4. *"If a king judges the poor with truth, His throne will be established forever"*. Proverbs 29:14.

Your reputation is what people think you are, but character is what God (and you) know you are.

- **Character is more than just talk.** Anyone can say that he has integrity, but action is the real indicator of character.
- **Talent is a gift, but character is a choice** (John C. Maxwell). Generally speaking, talent is something you're born with; you have little say in the matter. But character development and discipline is a choice you have to make each day.
- **Character brings lasting and enduring success.** People will not trust leaders whose character is faulty. Temporarily you may rise above your character limitations, but you won't be able to sustain the success without a strong character. Eventually, you will be seen for what you are. So, the counsel of the LORD is: don't just work to get to the top, work to build your character.

- **Knowledge will give you power, but character respect** (Bruce Lee). While knowledge empowers you to make informed decisions, it is a good character that will earn you respect.
- **When wealth is lost, nothing is lost; when health is lost, something is lost; when character is lost, all is lost** (Billy Graham). Good character is precious and losing it is a great loss, not money or any other material thing, not even your health.
- **Character is more important than intelligence** (Ralph Waldo Emerson). Regardless, if one is highly intelligent or not, character will focus a person to do the best they can with what they have. If the person has character, and high intelligence, character will inform the person to use their intelligence in a positive way. Intelligence without character is dangerous.

Though the world at large today cares little for righteousness and justice, the general principle of wisdom here still applies. Honesty is the best policy, and righteousness and justice are the best politics. This is not a time for complacency or compromise as a leader. It is a time for wisdom and courage. We need a return to righteousness and justice. We need this timeless truth in private life, family life, professional life, public life and political life. It is what it is and nothing else.

A Divine Sentence Is In The Lips Of The King

Proverbs 16:10 -12
"A divine sentence is in the lips of the king: his mouth transgresseth not in judgment. A just weight and balance are the LORD'S: all the weights of the bag are his work. It is an abomination to kings to commit wickedness: for the throne is established by righteousness."

The Bible elucidates inspired wisdom, deepest mysteries, and best policies by which thrones, and government stand firm, unshaken and established. In the inspired Book, the royal teacher in this text above made concise and profound statements about kings (all people in authority and positions of power) and the thrones on which they sit. Wise guidance and wisdom must be upon the lips of kings, a great sagacity and piercing judgement must be upon the lips of kings to discern dubious and difficult cases. This is one of the unique qualities of King Solomon adjured to be the wisest king on earth. Divine verdict or "divination" as the word signifies is like the oracle and what he says should be strictly true. This expresses and designs the operating standard for thrones, that kings and royal personalities on the thrones ought to speak as the oracles of God, but such is not found to be true in most people in positions of power and authority. Fathers and parents are to speak as the oracles of God in their families, equip and train their children with the capacity to speak the truth in every situation.

A good leader motivates, doesn't mislead or exploit his people, but speaks with divine authority, making right decisions that will advance the people and the land. In every situation and circumstance, the expression of the lips of kings ought to be divinely inspired. That is the scriptural standard for the content and manner of a king's speech. His mouth must not transgress in judgment. Kings and those who are in authority should act under the influence and inspiration of God so that their determinations in judgments and weighty matters, there may be no error or mistakes; they must possess the wisdom of God to discern clearly and administer justice in the land. In one instance, Solomon the wise king of Israel demonstrated this sagacity in his judging the two harlots and many people came from distant lands to hear and seek the wisdom of God. God's verdict must be on the lips of a king so that he will not err or go wrong in judgment.

It Is An Abomination To Kings To Commit Wickedness

The virtuous and royal character is that kings, rulers of people must demonstrate and manifest utmost hatred of all forms of wickedness as a lifestyle. Wicked behaviour, everything that is unrighteous and oppressive must be detestable to kings. Kings must abhor wickedness themselves together with their ministers and everyone working with them as written in Isaiah 32:

"Behold, a king shall reign in righteousness, and princes shall rule in judgment. And a man shall be as an hiding place from the wind, and a covert from the tempest; as rivers of water in a dry place, as the shadow of a great rock in a weary land".

Again, it is not enough to have righteous kings, rulers and leaders;

they must have helpers, princes working together with them who will also rule with justice. As a matter of fact, one major responsibility of kings, rulers and people in position of power and authority is to remove the wicked and wickedness from the land (Psalm 101). The prosperity of a civil government depends on the ability to execute righteousness and to deal with wickedness in the land. In this same spirit, kings and rulers must deploy their authority to others who will not subvert justice in the land.

For The Throne Is Established By Righteousness
The inspired wisdom now states that the throne is established by righteousness, what does this mean? The throne here does not mean only the royal seat, and this is the mistake we make in most cases, but it is the royal power and all its branches where it flows (Isaiah 32:1-4). It includes every person in government of a nation for instance that are involved in the administration, whether in making laws or executing same, all the officials and pillars behind the throne, businesses, and corporate organizations. It is not enough for the king to be righteous; all his officials must be righteous as well before the throne can be established. This is one dynamic of the throne's paradigm whereby all officials around the throne must be properly trained, schooled and trained in the inspired wisdom of integrity of heart and righteous behaviour for the mandate of thrones to be established. The throne, positions of leadership, government is established when it is rendered firm, made strong, secure, delivers good services to the people and justice to the land.

The inspired wisdom then states that the throne is best established (made strong, secure and firm) and sustained by righteousness, what does this mean? This practically has to do with the conduct and righteous behaviour of the king or anyone in a leadership position, the ability to do what is right and just on the thrones and to enforce the same. The lack of this type of righteous conduct and behaviour from households to businesses, corporate organizations, political power and government is what leads to chaos, instability and destruction of nations. This means righteous conduct, equity and justice of the king and all that are raised to any seat of influence, honour and service to humanity from households to the government of the nation.

Examples of Kings that Established Their Thrones in Righteousness

King Hezekiah is a good example of a king who reigned in righteousness, for it was written of him: *"And he did that which was right in the sight of the Lord, according to all that David his father did.He trusted in the Lord God of Israel; so that after him was none like him among all the kings of Judah, nor any that were before him. For he clave to the Lord, and departed not from following him, but kept his commandments, which the Lord commanded Moses. And the Lord was with him; and he prospered whithersoever he went forth:..."* 2 Kings 18:3, 5-7.

King Hezekiah had a righteous reign and good government. He had loyal princes such as Eliakim, Shebna the scribe and the elders of the priests who together with him administered justice and good governance in the land (2 Kings 19:2). King Josiah is another good example of a king who reigned in righteousness and established great reformation in the land, it is also written concerning him: *"And he did that which was right in the sight of the Lord, and walked in all the way of David his father, and turned not aside to the right hand or to the left."* 2 Kings 22:2

King Josiah's reign in Jerusalem is discussed in 2 Kings 22-23 and 2 Chronicles 34-35. The hallmark of Josiah's reign was his rediscovery of the Law of the Lord. King Josiah called for a time of national repentance. The Law was read to the people of the land, and a covenant made between the people and the Lord: *"The king stood by the pillar and made a covenant before the LORD, to walk after the LORD and to keep his commandments and his testimonies and his statutes with all his heart and all his soul, to perform the words of this covenant that were written in this book. And all the people joined in the covenant"* (2 kings 23:3). King Josiah carried out many reforms during his reign. The temple was cleansed from all objects of pagan worship, and the idolatrous high places in the land were demolished. King Josiah restored the true worship of God and removed mediums and witches from the land. It was written concerning him: *"Before him there was no king like him, who turned to the LORD with all his heart and with all his soul and with all his might, according to all the Law of Moses, nor did any like him arise after him."* (2 Kings 23:25)

Examples of Kings that Established Their Thrones in Wickedness

King Jeroboam and King Ahab are examples of kings that did the opposite by establishing their thrones in unrighteousness and wickedness. King Jeroboam, the son of Nebat was the first king of the divided kingdom of Israel. He had been promised great blessing and a continuing dynasty if he would follow the LORD (1 Kings 11:38). However, Jeroboam did not fully follow the LORD and obey Him. The king, set up two golden calves made for the people to worship and led the northern kingdom of Israel to an unprecedented sin and idolatry.

This sin of idolatry is recorded and referred to as "the sins of Jeroboam, the son of Nebat who taught Israel to sin" in the Bible. Even though Jeroboam started well, he did not end well. God raised him up as a king with great promises, but he used his position and influence as a king and plunged the entire nation into sin to the extent that many kings after him became ensnared by his evil foundation on the throne many years in the history of the nation. His wicked reign offers an example of the powerful influence of a king and the throne can have over others and the nation in a negative way for generations to come.

King Ahab is another evil king in the history of Israel (1 Kings 16: 29-34). It is written concerning him that he "did evil in the eyes of the LORD than any of those before him" (1 kings 16:30). Among the events that led to his wicked reign was his marriage to an evil woman, Jezebel the daughter of Ethbaal. Jezebel was a woman rooted in idolatry, cruelty, sorcery and mischief, she had a peculiar hostility against God's prophet and all that is good. The climax of the evil reign of Ahab was the murder of Naboth, a poor and an innocent man (1 Kings 21).

King Ahab coveted the vineyard belonging to Naboth and offered to buy it, but Naboth refused. While Ahab was despondent in his palace, Jezebel his wife arranged false witnesses against Naboth and arranged his death. Then, the king took over the vineyard of Naboth to himself. King Ahab sold himself to wickedness, abused his responsibility and influence, led the people into idolatry and shed innocent blood in the Land. Under him, prophets were killed, altars of God were destroyed, prophets of Baal and wicked people were promoted in the land. In the end it is written: "*there was never anyone like Ahab, who sold himself to do evil in the eyes of the Lord, urged on by Jezebel his wife.*

He behaved in the vilest manner going after idols" (1 Kings 21:25-26). Jezebel was thrown off the window, the king was judged by God, and all his descendants were cut off from the land.

Who Can Stand Up Under This Particular Process of God to Reform Nations?

"He that walketh righteously, and speaketh uprightly; he that despiseth the gain of oppressions, that shaketh his hands from holding of bribes, that stoppeth his ears from hearing of blood, and shutteth his eyes from seeing evil;
He shall dwell on high: his place of defence shall be the munitions of rocks: bread shall be given him; his waters shall be sure." Isaiah 33:1, 16

Without these characteristics, no throne can be sustained and this applies to all authority figures: a husband, father, religious, business and political leaders. Imputed righteousness or the righteousness of God through salvation in Christ Jesus makes us to have a right standing before God without condemnation and frees us from the law of sin and death, but not a substitute for Godly behaviour. We are saved by grace through faith in Christ Jesus, not of works and this prepares us to become oaks of righteousness with capacity to rebuild the waste places in every domain as kings and priest unto God.

Unfortunately, this type of Godly conduct and lifestyle is not being taught today. Even the Christian communities these days cares little about preparing, training and empowering people about doing what is right and just. We can gather great numbers of people into churches, but that has not and will not solve the problems of the nations until we intentionally, deliberately and strategically raise and mentor people with a throne culture of doing what is right and just.

The King By Judgement Establish The Land: But He That Receiveth Gifts Overthroweth It – Proverbs 29:4

This inspired wisdom again speaks of the effect of the actions of kings, rulers, and leadership in general in a nation and position of influence. It contrasts between a king who rules with justice and the one who operates based on dishonest gains and bribes. A leader who operates based on greed will bring pain to himself and his people. It again emphasis that leadership matters and that is why it is commanded that we should pray for leaders because their decisions affect the land. The greedy king overthrows his kingdom and nation, the same is true for any organization. By righteous decisions and impartial exercise of justice, kings and rulers build up, gives stability and restoration to their people and the land, but those whose delight and trademark practice it is to subvert judgement and take bribes destroys, tears down and demolishes the land.

The Sceptre of Righteousness

"Your throne, O God, is forever and ever; A sceptre of righteousness is the sceptre of Your kingdom. You love righteousness and hate wickedness; Therefore God, Your God, has anointed You. With the oil of gladness more than Your companions." Isaiah 9:7

A sceptre is a special rod or staff that a king or high official hold and essentially it is his instrument or symbol of power or authority. Christ's sceptre is a sceptre of righteousness, and this righteousness is doing what is right, just, honest and enforcing righteous rules. The best laws and constitutions are insignificant when they are badly administered. It requires great integrity and moral courage to withstand the temptations associated with thrones and leadership, yet there is tremendous power released when one is established in righteousness with the sceptre of righteousness. In the same way that a tree will grow taller and stronger when its roots grow deep, you will be stronger, rise higher and established when you are rooted and established in righteousness.

"Of the increase of his government and peace there shall be no end, upon the throne of David, and upon his kingdom, to order it, and to establish it with judgment and with justice from henceforth even forever. The zeal of the LORD of hosts will perform this." Isaiah 9:7

Operating on the thrones by doing what is right and just, the effect of righteous rulers on a nation and the benefits of enforcing righteousness is mentioned severally in the inspired word of God (Proverbs 29:2, 14:34). There is a great benefit for having righteous rulers with sceptres of righteousness on the thrones and courage to stir up people to do what is right and just by himself setting the standard. The nation will be built and stabilized rather being destroyed, the people will rejoice, wicked men will be removed, and the throne established.

This applies to families, religious and business organizations. A greedy ruler will ruin any organization all the time. To operate on the throne with the sceptre of righteousness starts by making a choice: a choice of what to love and what to hate. A choice to love righteousness and to hate wickedness (Psalm 101). Loving righteousness and hating wickedness releases His oil of gladness upon a ruler or a leader. "*I will set no wicked thing before mine eyes: I hate the work of them that turn aside; it shall not cleave to me. A froward heart shall depart from me: I will not know a wicked person. Whoso privily slandereth his neighbour, him will I cut off: him that hath an high look and a proud heart will not I suffer. Mine eyes shall be upon the faithful of the land, that they may dwell with me: he that walketh in a perfect way, he shall serve me. He that worketh deceit shall not dwell within my house: he that telleth lies shall not tarry in my sight. I will early destroy all the wicked of the land; that I may cut off all wicked doers from the city of the LORD.*" Psalm 101:3-8

The Sceptre of the Wicked – Isaiah 14:4-6

The sceptre of the wicked is a reference to the authority of the enemy and the rod of the wicked is used to exercise authority to inflict unjust treatment, but God will destroy the rod of the wicked among the nations. That you will take up this proverb against the king of Babylon, and say: "How the oppressor has ceased, the golden city ceased! The Lord has broken the staff of the wicked, the sceptre of the rulers. He who struck the people in wrath with a continual stroke, he who ruled the nations in anger, is persecuted and no one hinder.

PRAYERS:

- Open to me the gates of righteousness – Psalm 118:19.

- Give the king Your judgments, O God, And Your righteousness to the king's Son. He will judge Your people with righteousness, And Your poor with justice – Psalm 72:1-2.
- Psalm 101 – Make a commitment and determination to rule righteously.
- Psalm 125:3 – The sceptre of the wicked will not remain over the land allotted to the righteous.

14.

THE POWERS BEHIND THE THRONES

The king or the leader sitting on the throne is usually seen as the one who has the true and ultimate control. However, are there powers behind the throne? Powers behind the throne is a reference to people who are not the king or the leader on the throne, but who have great influence over the king or the person in a leadership position. They may be close family or courtiers with significant influence at royal courts or government. These influential persons could swing policy decisions through their personal connections and proximity to the thrones.

The phrase is usually used in the context of kings, thrones and government, to describe someone who is close to the king or official leader and has a great deal of influence over decision making. In politics, it often refers to a relative, aide, or subordinate of a political leader who exerts great influence on the de facto leader affecting decisions and policies through their influence on the leader. Kings, leaders, powerful men and women around the world all have personal counsellors, trusted aides and backroom confidants. These are insiders whose influence may be positive or negative, who may have personal agenda and ambitions of their own. Oftentimes, insiders with great influence on kings and leaders may be close family members.

The idea here is that kings and leaders rely to a surprising degree on the advice of close associates official or non-official and sometimes shady individuals who may decisively direct their actions and decisions. Some leaders even consult and confide in personal astrologers, others may turn for help to inexperienced people who are unfit to serve in any capacity of leadership, and yet they have the ear of kings, leaders and many people in authority. These influencers may take advantage of a weak leader to usurp and manipulate the powers of the throne for their selfish interest and evil agendas.

Understanding these powers behind the thrones is crucial to gaining an understanding of power dynamics on the throne and how it affects decision-making and subsequently the entire kingdom or nation.

Understanding these dynamics of influence is important for those seeking to be involved in the complexities of power, and for those who seek to establish righteousness and justice in the land. Therefore, as part of the strategies to establish righteousness and justice, we need to pay attention to the powers behind the thrones and the dynamics of the influence exerted by behind-the-thrones advisers and confidants who have the ear of kings, leaders and government officials.

Jezebel, The Queen of Israel

Jezebel, was the wife of King Ahab who ruled the kingdom of Israel. After her marriage to King Ahab, Jezebel emerged as the power behind the throne. As a woman seeking even more power, she sought to destroy those who questioned her, and most of the prophets of Yahweh were murdered at her request. Those who escaped went into hiding. Jezebel was the daughter of Ethbaal, a king and the priest of Baal. When Jezebel married King Ahab, she brought her foreign gods and influenced the king to worship her god, Baal, a nature god.

"In the thirty-eighth year of Asa king of Judah, Ahab the son of Omri became king over Israel; and Ahab the son of Omri reigned over Israel in Samaria twenty-two years. Now Ahab the son of Omri did evil in the sight of the Lord, more than all who were before him. And it came to pass, as though it had been a trivial thing for him to walk in the sins of Jeroboam the son of Nebat, that he took as wife Jezebel the daughter of Ethbaal, king of the Sidonians; and he went and served Baal and worshiped him. Then he set up an altar for Baal in the temple of Baal, which he had built in Samaria. And Ahab made a wooden image. Ahab did more to provoke the Lord God of Israel to anger than all the kings of Israel who were before him". 1 Kings 16:29-33

A woman of fierce energy, she tried to destroy those who opposed her; most of the prophets of Yahweh were killed at her command. Under her malevolent influence, King Ahab established altars of Baal and pagan rituals, which lead God to inflict a three-year drought in a land of Israel. Her influence was in many respects very disastrous to the nation of Israel, she prompted the internal conflict that plagued Israel for decades.

The last vicious act attributed to Jezebel is recorded in 1 Kings 21:5–16. Next to King Ahab's palace was a vineyard which belonged to Naboth. The king desired and coveted Naboth's vineyard, but Naboth did not let go of his inheritance. When Naboth refused to part with his vineyard, Jezebel falsely manipulated witnesses against him. He was charged with blaspheming God and the king and Naboth an innocent was stoned to death. Jezebel's name became synonymous with evil and wicked powers behind the throne. At the end Jezebel was brought to a shameful death.

Elymas, The Sorcerer

Upon Paul's conversion to Christianity, he had a mandate and vision to minister to kings and those in authority. Jesus told Ananias in Acts 9:15, "**Go, for he is a chosen instrument of mine to carry My name before the Gentiles and kings and the children of Israel.**" Eventually, Paul and Barnabas became leaders in the church in Antioch when the Holy Spirit told the community to send them on mission. They went to Cyprus and started preaching directly to the centres of power. They spoke first to the Jewish leaders and then to the Roman governor of the area. But when Paul was teaching Sergius Paulus, the Roman governor he encountered opposition from Elymas, a sorcerer who obviously is a close adviser to the governor and has captured him and his government by mystical powers (state capture).

"Now when they had gone through the island to Paphos, they found a certain sorcerer, a false prophet, a Jew whose name was Bar-Jesus, who was with the proconsul, Sergius Paulus, an intelligent man. This man called for Barnabas and Saul and sought to hear the word of God. But Elymas the sorcerer (for so his name is translated) withstood them, seeking to turn the proconsul away from the faith. Then Saul, who also is called Paul, filled with the Holy Spirit, looked intently at him and said, "O full of all deceit and all fraud, you son of the devil, you enemy of all righteousness, will you not cease perverting the straight ways of the Lord? And now, indeed, the hand of the Lord is upon you, and you shall be blind, not seeing the sun for a time."And immediately a dark mist fell on him, and he went around seeking someone to lead him by the hand. Then the proconsul believed, when he saw what had

been done, being astonished at the teaching of the Lord". Acts
13:6-12

Lessons.

- It is instructive that the governor was an intelligent man, yet he submitted to a sorcerer as his confidant. This was an important leader responsible for an entire province. The point is that many important kings, leaders no matter how intelligent they may be can still be subject to control and manipulations. Elymas, the sorcerer had emerged as the power behind the throne and captured the governor and the government.
- The governor called Paul to hear the word of God and to learn the right ways of doing things, but Elymas withstood Paul and sought to turn the governor from the faith.
- It is worth noting that when you seek to establish kings, leaders and thrones in righteousness you may become a threat to an adviser with mystical power. You may be talking to a king or governor while actually you are battling against magicians and may have to push against powers that need to be brought down in order to establish the throne in righteousness.
- The sorcerer Elymas was cursed with blindness, paving the way to teach and prompting the Governor, Sergius Paulus to embrace the truth and the right ways of God. In other words, we need to know how to deal with evil powers behind the throne in order to establish the kings and thrones in righteousness.

Conclusion

The point here is that, while the throne is certainly a symbol of power and authority, the power dynamics of sitting on it are complex and multidimensional. When we understand these dynamics, we will be informed about the challenges and responsibilities that come with sitting on the throne as a powerful symbol of governance. The dynamics of influence is a major factor when it comes to a king or a leader doing what is right on the throne in many instances. Understanding the dynamics of influence is therefore critical for those seeking to steer the complexities of power in order to establish righteousness and justice in any territory, domains of influence and nations.

15.

RULING IN THE FEAR OF THE LORD

The Concept of Ruling in the Fear of God

The concept of ruling in the fear of God is a timeless and universal principle for effective leadership, good governance and sustainable development. Because leadership is complex and saddled with great responsibilities, it requires strong commitment to sound ethics and morality together with other strategic leadership skills to champion sustainable transformation of kingdoms and nations. Ruling in the fear of God stems from the fact that a king's or a leader's first allegiance must be to God, they must realise the Most High rules in the affairs of men and thus worship Him.

Fundamental Components of Ruling in the Fear of God

- Recognition, total submission and complete allegiance to God as the supreme authority that governs the universe and rules in the affairs of men.
- Commitment to ethical and moral behaviour, set high standard of moral behaviour for himself and followers as well. Lee Kuan Yew of Singapore did exactly the same to transform his nation.
- Acknowledging that they are accountable first and foremost to God and then to the people that God has graciously raised them up to lead. The summary of a good king or leader is that he did what was right before God always.
- Understand and hold their authority as a trust from God for the good of the land.
- Commitment to fairness, equity and justice without compromise.

The Fear of God Versus the Fear of Men

The fear of God means giving God your undivided attention, reverence and utmost commitment to carry out His commandments always, it is described as the whole duty of man: *"**Let us hear the conclusion of the whole matter: Fear God, and keep his commandments: for this is the whole duty of man.**"* (Ecclesiastes 12:13). The fear of man on the other hand is the quest for the approval of other people which negate the fear of God. The fear of man competes against the fear of God and a key implication of an utmost fear of God is to lay aside the fear of men in all ramifications. We all experience the fear of other people's approval and most people don't understand how serious this can be. The fear of man can incapacitate even a great king or leader. That is why the Bible teaches us, *"**The fear of man lays a snare, but whoever trusts in the Lord is safe**"* (Proverbs 29:25). Snares are dangerous. It refers to traps that the hunters use to catch birds or animals.

To Fear God is What the Lord Your God Require of You

The fear of God is what your God require of you, it is a command to fear God supremely and seek God's approval than mortal men's approval and to choose the fear of God is for your own good and success.

> *"**And now, Israel, what doth the Lord thy God require of thee, but to fear the Lord thy God, to walk in all his ways, and to love him, and to serve the Lord thy God with all thy heart and with all thy soul,To keep the commandments of the Lord, and his statutes, which I command thee this day for thy good?**"* (Deuteronomy 10:12-13).
>
> *"**And fear not them which kill the body, but are not able to kill the soul: but rather fear him which is able to destroy both soul and body in hell**"* (Matthew 10:28).

Trusting God especially in any given leadership position and throne assignment is safe, but fearing men in whatever degree is a snare. The orientation of King Saul when he succumbed to the fear of men and the consequences thereof should teach every king and leader to choose the fear of God and abstain from the fear of men. King Saul was set up for success.

He was chosen by God, anointed and blessed; he should have been a great king. God gave King Saul, a clear command: destroy Amalek and bring total judgment against the Amalekites, but instead, Saul took some of their best livestock as plunder and let their king live (1 Samuel 15). King Saul lost God's favour and was rejected as king due to his disobedience, because he feared the people and not God. For long life and prosperity on the thrones, kings and leaders must understand that they must conquer the fear of men, otherwise the fear of men will destroy them. The LORD rejected Saul as a king because he feared the people and obeyed their voice instead of the commandments of God (1 Samuel 15).

1 Samuel 15:24-26
And Saul said unto Samuel, I have sinned: for I have transgressed the commandment of the Lord, and thy words: because I feared the people, and obeyed their voice.
Now therefore, I pray thee, pardon my sin, and turn again with me, that I may worship the Lord.
And Samuel said unto Saul, I will not return with thee: for thou hast rejected the word of the Lord, and the Lord hath rejected thee from being king over Israel.

I had the privilege of ministering to a king of no small territory, who according to him was succumbed to the fear of his people for ten years on the throne. He knew what God wanted him to do as a king, but for the fear of what the people will do to him he was hindered and incapacitated for ten years in bondage to the fear of men. At the point of losing everything, he cried unto God and made a commitment and chose to fear God rather men; and after a period of prayers and fasting in the palace, the almighty God delivered him from the fear of men. In another palace of a king, I shared on the fear of God as a timeless principle of long life and prosperity on the throne. The king knelt down and asked to be prayed for and anointed. After the exercise, he confessed that he has been operating on the throne all these years in fear of men and said from that day he received boldness to operate on the throne.

The Last Words of King David

Ruling in the fear of God was the last will and testament of King David. The last words of great and good men are thought worthy to be in a special manner remarked and remembered. David being a royal prophet declared in the last days of his reign as he was inspired by the Spirit of God:

2 Samuel 23:1-4
Now these be the last words of David. David the son of Jesse said, and the man who was raised up on high, the anointed of the God of Jacob, and the sweet psalmist of Israel, said,
The Spirit of the Lord spake by me, and his word was in my tongue.
The God of Israel said, the Rock of Israel spake to me, He that ruleth over men must be just, ruling in the fear of God.
And he shall be as the light of the morning, when the sun riseth, even a morning without clouds; as the tender grass springing out of the earth by clear shining after rain.

What a profound and powerful instructions by a great king, a man after God's heart!

He That Rule Over Men Must Be Just

This is the character every king and leader among men in any sphere of influence must possess, administering justice to their subjects. This character was found in David. And David reigned over all Israel; and David executed judgment and justice unto all his people (2 Samuel 8:15) and his last words is hereby written for all kings and leaders in every generation. It is a known fact that this divine construct to bring peace and prosperity to the nations is grossly compromised today in our society. As God's representatives over your kingdom or domains of influence, this profound principle must not be a rhetoric guideline, but one that is established firmly in the heart. It should manifest in your dispositions and actions on any matter be it little or big.

Ruling in the Fear of God

Acting with the mind-set to honour and glorify God on the throne to whom they are accountable, kings and leaders should rule in the fear of God and not the fear of men. The fear of the LORD is more of being subject to His Lordship and obedience to His sovereign will in all areas of our lives and always. The Fear of the Lord is not the fear that grips you when you suddenly come face to face with an intimidating and frightening object or situation. Proverbs 8:13 says:

Proverbs 8:13
The fear of the LORD is to hate evil: pride, and arrogance, and the evil way, and the forward mouth, do I hate

He shall be as light of the morning, when the Sun rise. Try and picture having leaders like this in our lives and all of us who are in any position of leadership at all; in our homes, different positions in our churches, in our workplaces, in our communities and nations administering justice and ruling in the fear of God. **As the tender grass springing out of the Earth by clear shining after rain**. Imagine just authorities leading in the fear of God in all kinds of high positions – presidents, prime ministers, kings and queens, legislators and judges – what blessings will flow to the leadership, the people and the nation. As we think of leading marriages, leading homes, leading in different capacities in workplaces, marketplaces, in schools, in our communities and in government of nations, we need to bear in mind the two golden rules: to be just and to rule in the fear of God.

Jeremiah 23:5, 6
Behold, the days come, saith the Lord, that I will raise unto David a righteous Branch, and a King shall reign and prosper, and shall execute judgment and justice in the earth.
In his days Judah shall be saved, and Israel shall dwell safely: and this is his name whereby he shall be called, The Lord Our Righteousness

Specific Guidance to Rule in the Fear of God
Understand that ruling in the fear of God is deeply a personal and spiritual journey that you need to set your priority in order to achieve and herewith are some specific guidance.

- Worship and prayer – prioritise personal relationship with God with prayers. Establish prayer altar in your palace or domain of influence and don't compromise on your faith and responsibility to publicly proclaim your faith in God.

- Seek wisdom and pursue understanding – the fear of the Lord is the beginning of wisdom. Wisdom is better than weapon of war, make sure you prioritise wisdom.
- Serve and do not lord over God's people – serve as a steward of the authority and resources entrusted into your hands.
- Integrity – Be honest with yourself and others, be sincere, transparent and shun corruption and abuse of power.
- Humble yourself under the hand of God and don't think highly of yourself.
- Lead by example – your personal life speaks volumes. Be a value-driven leader
- Continuous growth and development, do not stop learning and do everything to associate with people of sound wisdom.
- Skill development – David led Israel by integrity and skilfulness of his hands. You need to keep developing your skills and adding values to your life with competence
- Defend the poor and the needy – a king that defend the poor and the needy, his throne will be established forever.
- Do not give your strength to what destroys kings and do not give yourself to strong drinks.

The Conclusion of the Whole Matter – Ecclesiastes 12:13, 14

The teacher discussed every endeavour of man under the sun and came to the conclusion that the whole of a man is to fear God and obey His commandment. It is a call to set the fear of God as a priority and lay aside the fear of men, for it is worth it to obey the voice of God and to live as one preparing for judgment and eternity.

"Let us hear the conclusion of the whole matter: Fear God, and keep his commandments: for this is the whole duty of man. For God shall bring every work into judgment, with every secret thing, whether it be good, or whether it be evil"(Ecclesiastes 12:13, 14).

Prayers – Teach me thy way, O Lord; I will walk in thy truth: unite my heart to fear thy name. Psalms 86:11

16.

THE POWER OF WISDOM

What is Wisdom?

The Greek word for wisdom is Sophia, and Hebrew Chokmah which means experience, shrewdness, knowledge, and the ability to make the right choices and take the right decisions. Wisdom also means sagacity, discernment, sound judgment and deep insight. Wisdom is divine insight on how to solve a problem, how to conduct your affairs to attain enduring success and how to apply acquired knowledge in workable manners for your benefit and the good of others. Wisdom sees the big picture and other parts as they relate to achieving the main focus and goal. In whatever position or situation you find yourself, you have to make decisions and decisions can be difficult to make, especially decisions that have to do with the destiny of a nation and many people. We are all faced with decisions every single day and we need God's wisdom to make the right decisions and choices.

King Solomon Empowered with Wisdom

At the beginning of his reign, King Solomon sought after true wisdom from God to administer justice and righteousness on the throne, for his father taught him the importance of true wisdom and the counsel of God. The LORD appeared in a dream by night to Solomon as a young and inexperienced king and said to him "Ask! What shall I give you?"

And now, O LORD my God, thou hast made thy servant king instead of David my father: and I am but a little child: I know not how to go out or come in. And thy servant is in the midst of thy people which thou hast chosen, a great people, that cannot be numbered nor counted for multitude. Give therefore thy servant an understanding heart to judge thy people, that I may discern between good and bad: for who is able to judge this thy so great a people? 1 Kings 3:7-9

And it pleased the LORD that Solomon asked and prayed for wisdom instead of long life, for riches or for the life of his enemies that God gave him wisdom, riches, honour, conquest, peaceful reign, long life and prosperity like no other king.

"And the speech pleased the Lord, that Solomon had asked this thing. And God said unto him, Because thou hast asked this thing, and hast not asked for thyself long life; neither hast asked riches for thyself, nor hast asked the life of thine enemies; but hast asked for thyself understanding to discern judgment; Behold, I have done according to thy words: lo, I have given thee a wise and an understanding heart; so that there was none like thee before thee, neither after thee shall any arise like unto thee. And I have also given thee that which thou hast not asked, both riches, and honour: so that there shall not be any among the kings like unto thee all thy days".

By this wisdom King Solomon set up the best administration ever in the kingdom, made wise decisions for his kingdom, chose the right people to administer the kingdom with him, carried out the last instructions of King David and administer justice between disputing parties. He however did not finish well because his heart was turned away from God by strange women which is another dynamic a leader must guide against to finish strong on the throne.

Wisdom is the Supreme Principal Thing

So many books have been written about success and how to attain success, but significant success still evades many. Still, so many people are living in deep frustration, pains from divorces and family troubles, depression, failure, poverty, and mediocrity. One main cause of this is the lack of wisdom to handle situations and circumstances among others. The inspired book is very clear about this by declaring wisdom as the principal thing to acquire in order to function effectively and efficiently in whatever role or assignment given to you under this heaven.

Wisdom is the principal thing; therefore get wisdom. And in all your getting, get understanding -Prov. 4:7 NKJV.

Wisdom is supreme, it is the instrument to solve many problems in every society and in all spheres of influence. Life in its totality is about solving problems and throne's assignment is about providing solutions to many difficult issues and challenges in the society. Every challenge, difficulty, and circumstance we encounter in life requires wisdom. . It is expected of kings and all those in authority to operate in the manifold wisdom of God which is a wisdom frequency that is far above ordinary human wisdom because thrones are created to proffer solutions. And this is true for every man or woman, husband, father, leader (spiritual, corporate/business, and political). People make terrible mistakes due to lack of wisdom and many have ruined their lives, destroyed their marriages and families, businesses and enterprise, wreak havoc in their domains and nations because they lack this crucial tool that is called wisdom.

The Components of Wisdom
Wisdom has components boldly written out in Proverbs 8:12-21

"I, wisdom, dwell with prudence, and find out knowledge and discretion. The fear of the Lord is to hate evil; Pride and arrogance and the evil way and the perverse mouth I hate. Counsel is mine, and sound wisdom; I am understanding, I have strength. By me kings reign, and rulers decree justice. By me princes rule, and nobles, All the judges of the earth. I love those who love me, and those who seek me diligently will find me. Riches and honor are with me, Enduring riches and righteousness. My fruit is better than gold, yes, than fine gold, and my revenue than choice silver. I traverse the way of righteousness, In the midst of the paths of justice, that I may cause those who love me to inherit wealth, that I may fill their treasuries."

Here wisdom reveals: who she is, what she discovers, what she has, what she hates, what she loves, who she dwells with, what she does, what she produces and what you gain if you possess wisdom.

- She is understanding.
- She discovers knowledge and discretion.
- She has counsel, strength, riches, honor, length of days, righteousness and enduring wealth.
- She hates pride, arrogance, evil, wickedness and a perverse mouth.
- She loves everyone that love her and diligently seek her.
- She dwells with prudence.
- She produces fruits that cannot be compared to precious metals of silver or gold.
- She is life unto them that find her and they will obtain favor of the LORD (Vs.35).
- She is a tree of life to them that lay hold upon her…Prov. 3:18a.

The Seven Pillars of Wisdom – Prov. 9:1

In Proverbs, we understand that the house of wisdom has seven pillars:

Wisdom has built her house; she has hewn out her seven pillars (Prov. 9:1).

- The Fear of the LORD: Deep reverence and awe for God's love, power and authority
- Instructions: detail information about how something should be done or operated
- Knowledge: facts, information, and skills acquired through experience or education
- Understanding: the ability to understand something; comprehension, a mental grasp
- Discretion: the freedom to decide what should be done in a particular situation, tactfulness, prudence
- Counsel: advice, guidance, direction to make right decision
- Reproof: rebuke, reprimand; an expression of disapproval.

By Me Kings Reign and Princes Decree Justice

The major resource to operate on the thrones is God's creative wisdom and witty inventions. This wisdom helps to make good decisions in your life, to lead others successfully as well and proffer bold initiatives and solutions as kings and leaders in any domain. Wisdom is very important in running the affairs of life.

> *I wisdom dwell with prudence and find out knowledge of witty inventions.*
> *The fear of the LORD is to hate evil: pride, and arrogancy, and the evil way, and the froward mouth, do I hate.*
> *Counsel is mine, and sound wisdom: I am understanding; I have strength.*
> *By me kings reign, and princes decree justice*
> *By me princes rule, and nobles, even all the judges of the earth.*
> *I love them that love me; and those that seek me early shall find me.*

Unfortunately, kings and great men and women both in history and the contemporary world, ministers of God, corporate and business leaders, political office bearers, civil leaders, men and women who have reached the highest pinnacle of fame have been ruined because they failed to hearken to the cry of wisdom. This lack of wisdom shows up in disobedience to God's will, inordinate ambition, envy, sexual immorality, corruption, inordinate quest for political power, and all vices. To operate on the thrones and be successful, you must possess wisdom consistently because the righteous execution of your mandate, assignment and responsibilities on the thrones depends on the wisdom of God which many kings and leaders despise to their own peril and the destruction of their nations and people as well. Great families, kingdoms and nations have leaders blessed with this kind of wisdom. Abraham was set to be a great family and a great nation because he possessed the wisdom to teach, train and command his household to walk in the counsels of God to do what is right and just. Great families have fathers who operate with the wisdom of God and set examples for their children after them and make them great. The greatness of a nation depends on rulers with wisdom to enact and enforce righteousness and justice for all, and this kind of wisdom comes from the inspired instructions in the word of God.

True Wisdom for Godly Kings and all People in Authority

The wisdom of those in authority is to detest evil and anyone who sits on any throne without the true wisdom of God will eventually become a tyrant. In the inspired book of Proverbs, the teacher taught that by wisdom kings reign and princes decree righteous laws. Unfortunately, many people operate without this true wisdom on the thrones, and that is why many kings, princes and leaders manifest wickedness and pervasions on their thrones. **Today, nations and kingdoms of the world are groaning in fear, turmoil, chaos and unfathomable deficiencies and difficulties, killings, division, hatred, race problems, wars, and destruction for lack of wisdom in their leaders**.

Those who operate on the thrones must rule rightly and justly by wisdom and discretion which comes from God. Wisdom is so crucial in operating on the thrones that a poor and a wise child with wisdom is said to be better than an old and foolish king who does not possess wisdom (Eccl. 4:13). Today we need leaders to proffer kingdom solutions to society's problems as we come to embrace and understand the power and the dynamics of thrones. The throne paradigm is to train and mentor men and women equipped with the capacity and audacity to challenge the status quo and bring dynamic solutions to transform their domains through the power of wisdom. At the beginning of his reign, King Solomon sought after true wisdom from God to administer justice and righteousness on the throne, for his father taught him the importance of true wisdom and the counsel of God. The LORD appeared in a dream by night to Solomon as a young and inexperienced king and said to him "Ask! What shall I give you?"

And now, O LORD my God, thou hast made thy servant king instead of David my father: and I am but a little child: I know not how to go out or come in. And thy servant is in the midst of thy people which thou hast chosen, a great people, that cannot be numbered nor counted for multitude. Give therefore thy servant an understanding heart to judge thy people, that I may discern between good and bad: for who is able to judge this thy so great a people? 1 kings 3:7-9

And it pleased the LORD that Solomon asked and prayed for wisdom instead of long life, for riches or for the life of his enemies that God gave him wisdom, riches, honor, conquest, peaceful reign, long life and prosperity like no other king.

And the speech pleased the Lord, that Solomon had asked this thing. And God said unto him, Because thou hast asked this thing, and hast not asked for thyself long life; neither hast asked riches for thyself, nor hast asked the life of thine enemies; but hast asked for thyself understanding to discern judgment; Behold, I have done according to thy words: lo, I have given thee a wise and an understanding heart; so that there was none like thee before thee, neither after thee shall any arise like unto thee. And I have also given thee that which thou hast not asked, both riches, and honour: so that there shall not be any among the kings like unto thee all thy days.

By this wisdom, King Solomon set up the best administration ever in the kingdom, made wise decisions for his kingdom, chose the right people to administer the kingdom with him, carried out the last instructions of King David and administered justice between disputing parties. He however did not finish well because his heart was turned away from God by strange women which is another dynamic a leader must guide against to finish strong on the throne.

The Knowledge of Wisdom
Wisdom teaches kings, leaders and everyone who desires to be significantly successful on the thrones very many important principles to fulfil their throne's mandate and finish well.

- Wisdom teaches kings the important principle of what brings honour to kings and leaders is to search out matters diligently, with no assumption (Prov. 25:3).
- Wisdom teaches wise kings and leaders the crucial issue of dealing with the wicked in the land (Prov. 20:8,26).
- Wisdom teaches kings and leaders that mercy and truth will preserve them and that lovingkindness will uphold their thrones

(Prov. 20:28).
- Wisdom teaches kings and leaders the benefits of faithfully judging the poor of the land thereby establishing their thrones (Prov. 29:14; 31:8-9).
- Wisdom teaches kings and leaders the importance of relating and surrounding themselves with good men in the kingdom with gracious speech and capacity to speak truth to them (Prov. 14:35; 16:13; 22:11). It is critical that when you are in a position of authority, you set your mind to hear those who will speak honestly, frankly and wisely to you. To learn to hear and embrace the truth rather than flattery because most princes and leaders are brought low by those who speak to soothe them than those who speak the truth.
- Wisdom teaches kings and leaders many things to avoid in order to establish the land and their subjects. Kings must avoid bribes otherwise they will overthrow the land (Prov. 29:4). Bribery and corruption is a strong and common temptations when it comes to the thrones and by this many leaders have been brought low.
- Wisdom teaches kings to avoid wine and intoxicating drinks so that they will not pervert justice in the land (Prov. 31:4,5).
- Wisdom teaches kings and leaders not to give their strength to whorish women and things that easily destroy kings (Prov. 31:3).
- Wisdom teaches kings and leaders to remove wicked counsellors from before them in order to establish their thrones (Prov. 25:5).
- Wisdom teaches kings and leaders about dangerous promises (Prov. 6:1-5).

The Power of Wisdom

The power of wisdom lies in its ability to empower you to run the affairs of life, take the right decisions and handle complex situations effectively.

Wisdom Makes One Wise Person More Powerful Than Ten Rulers in a City – Prov.7:19 NIV

The Teacher tells us that wisdom brings strength and power with it. Wisdom is better than ten valiant, physically strong, leaders, or generals, and their men. When you prioritize your goals to pursue wisdom more than anything else, you will gain strength and power more than your contemporary (Daniel 1:17-20).

Wisdom is a powerful tool for national transformation. It has the power to make kings, men and women, civil and all rulers great and their kingdoms great with peace and prosperity. Wherever and whenever wisdom is absent, there will be chaos and crisis: this is true for families as well as other domains of influence and nations. Wisdom empowers you to excel above your peers. God is excellent. He wants you to excel because excellence attracts you before great men and the spirit of excellence empowers you to accomplish your throne mandate.

Wisdom Empowers You With Understanding

Fundamentally, wisdom will empower you with understanding: specifically to understand differences; whether the differences are between good and evil, true and false, right and wrong. Whatever purpose you have been designed by God to fulfil on the throne, wisdom will empower you to fulfil it. Great purpose and assignment require great wisdom.

Wisdom Empowers You With Discernment

The ability to know the difference between right and wrong, the ability to choose what is good above what is evil is critical for all throne assignments. With wisdom comes discernment. Discernment empowers you to see evil when it is disguised as good. Discernment empowers you to perceive and overcome deception. Skilful deceivers and manipulators always infiltrate the corridors of power to deceive and dissuade the leader who is not properly armed with discernment.

Wisdom Empowers With Defence and Protect You

When you have wisdom, you are empowered with security. A person without wisdom is defenceless and open to attack from the enemy, but a person with wisdom is equipped with security and well-defended. How does wisdom protect you? Wisdom helps you to see danger from afar and stay out of it.

"For wisdom is a defence, and money is a defence: but the excellency of knowledge is that wisdom giveth life to them that have it. Eccl. 7:12

Wisdom Empowers You to Make Wealth

Wisdom is a deep well of wealth. Through a careful study of the life of Solomon, you will discover that wealth came to him continually because of wisdom.

"Riches and honour are with me, yea durable riches and righteousness." Prov. 8:18

Wisdom Empowers You With Direction

There is no misery that is as complicated as been confused, not knowing who you are, your purpose and what to do. Wisdom empowers you to discover your purpose, to pursue it and fulfil it. Without wisdom life remains a mystery. It is wisdom that shows you the route to your destiny.

*"**Wisdom is profitable to direct**." Eccl. 10:10*

Wisdom Empowers You With Creativity

With wisdom is the power of witty inventions. Wisdom empowers creativity which is the wisdom to turn ideas into reality and raw materials into finished products.

"I wisdom dwell with prudence, and find out the knowledge of witty inventions." Prov. 8:12

Wisdom empowers you with new ways of doing things.

Wisdom Empowers You to Reign on the Earth

Through the grace of redemption, all believers are kings and priests ordained to reign on the earth. One of the frameworks to rule and to reign on the earth is the power of wisdom: no one can truly reign successfully on the earth without wisdom. The height of your greatness and the increase of your influence or kingdom is determined by the greatness of your wisdom. Jesus is the power and the wisdom of God.

***By me kings reign, and princes decree justice.** Proverbs 8:15*

Wisdom Empowers You to Build Your Family and Sustainable Relationships

It takes wisdom, understanding and knowledge to build a successful marriage and family relationships. In most cases, marital crises around the world are caused by lack of wisdom.

"Through wisdom a house is built, and by understanding it is established; by knowledge the rooms are filled with all precious and pleasant riches." Prov. 24:3, 4

Wisdom is the true building block for a successful marriage and family. Many things that cause misunderstandings in marriages and families are things that can be resolved by the power of wisdom. In the spirit of wisdom, you understand you must put your marriage and family first and you know by wisdom it is better to win your partner than to win an argument but lose your partner. Wisdom teaches kings not to give their strength to wrong marriages and relationships.

Wisdom Empowers You with Strength

Wise warriors are mightier than strong ones because the wise prevail through the power of wisdom.

"A wise man is strong, yes, a man of knowledge increases strength; for by wise counsel you will wage your own war, and in a multitude of counselors there is safety." Prov. 24: 5, 6

A man of great power and strength is a man who is wise and has knowledge; for real power and strength are on the inside, not the outside. It comes from the ability to understand many things and to make good, precise and prompt decisions. Anyone who prioritizes the importance of good counsel and guidance will enhance their own power and strength to deal with challenges.

Wisdom Empowers Your Promotion

You don't have to bring others down for you to get to the top as many people do to attain leadership positions, wisdom will see to it that you are lifted up and promoted.

Exalt her, and she shall promote thee. Prov. 4:8

God will not give you what is beyond your capacity to handle, otherwise you will crumble. It is wisdom that lifted Daniel to be given one hundred and twenty-seven provinces to administer:

"There is a man in your kingdom in whom is the Spirit of the Holy God. And in the days of your father, light and understanding and wisdom, like the wisdom of the gods, were found in him; and King Nebuchadnezzar your father—your father the king—made him chief of the magicians, astrologers, Chaldeans, and soothsayers. Inasmuch as an excellent spirit, knowledge, understanding, interpreting dreams, solving riddles, and explaining enigmas were found in this Daniel, whom the king named Belteshazzar, now let Daniel be called, and he will give the interpretation." Daniel 5:11, 12.

It is the power of wisdom that lifted Joseph from prison to become prime minister in Egypt, the greatest economy in his own time:

And Pharaoh said to his servants, "Can we find such a one as this, a man in whom is the Spirit of God?" Then Pharaoh said to Joseph, "Inasmuch as God has shown you all this, there is no one as discerning and wise as you. You shall be over my house, and all my people shall be ruled according to your word; only in regard to the throne will I be greater than you." And Pharaoh said to Joseph, "See, I have set you over all the land of Egypt." Genesis 41:38-41

Wisdom Empowers Productivity

Solomon prioritized wisdom which is evident in his productivity, the works he produced and his administrative sagacity. He was productive in many natural areas like writing proverbs, songs, and knowledge of plants, trees, and animal kingdom (1 Kings 4:30-34).

Other Benefits of Godly Wisdom

King Solomon wrote so many things about the benefits of wisdom and the whole of the Holy Bible is about the wisdom of God. Recommended study: Proverbs chapter 1-8.

Happy is the man who finds wisdom, And the man who gains understanding;
For her proceeds are better than the profits of silver, And her gain than fine gold. She is more precious than rubies, And all the things you may desire cannot compare with her.
Length of days is in her right hand, In her left hand riches and honor.
Her ways are ways of pleasantness, And all her paths are peace.
She is a tree of life to those who take hold of her,
And happy are all who retain her. Proverbs 3:13-18

How Do You Acquire and Develop Wisdom?

- It takes the fear of God to access the wisdom of God – Prov. 9:10; Psa. 1119:97-100.
- Solomon taught us that true wisdom is from God. And James has taught us that if we lack wisdom, we need to ask God.
- Proverbs also taught us the need to prioritize our goals to pursue wisdom diligently with the whole of our heart: for wisdom is better than all other things.
- We acquire wisdom by meditating on the Book of The Law day and Night – Prov. 1:13.
- We acquire wisdom when we prepare our hearts to seek God.
- Seek and ask wise counsel – Prov. 12:15.
- Ask for wisdom (James 1:5). Like King Solomon, with humility, you need to acknowledge your lack of wisdom and ask for it. As recorded in the Bible, God gave Solomon wisdom in abundance when he humbled himself and asked God for wisdom.

Wisdom is available for every man and every woman. You can have this wisdom by humbling yourself to truly love and fear God; by praying and asking for wisdom, and by studying wisdom in the word of God.

Conclusion

The pursuit of wisdom must become a priority in your life because wisdom will protect, prosper, promote and empower you to excel in your life, your marriage, in your workplace, in the marketplace, in your throne's assignment, in governance and whatever area you need to exercise good and sound judgment.

'For the LORD gives wisdom; from his mouth come knowledge and understanding. He stores up success for the upright; He is a shield for those who live with integrity so that he may guard the paths of justice and protect the way of his faithful followers. Then you will understand righteousness, justice, and integrity, every good path.' (Proverbs 2:6-9 CSB)

17.

COURAGE TO OPERATE ON THE THRONES

First Thing First: Be of Good Courage

At the commissioning of Joshua to take over the leadership of God's people from Moses, God commands Joshua to take courage: All leaders need courage and it is sometimes a matter of life and death in certain situations. Courage is one of the keys to great leadership, that is why God started by building courage in the life of Joshua.

"Moses My servant is dead. Now therefore, arise, go over this Jordan, you and all this people, to the land which I am giving to them – the children of Israel. Every place that the sole of your foot will tread upon I have given you, as I said to Moses
Be strong and of good courage, for to this people you shall divide as an inheritance the land which I swore to their fathers to give them".
Only be strong and very courageous, that you may observe to do according to all the law which Moses My servant commanded you; do not turn from it to the right hand or to the left, that you may prosper wherever you go.
Have I not commanded you? Be strong and of good courage; do not be afraid, nor be dismayed, for the Lord your God is with you wherever you go." Joshua 1: 2,3, 6, 7 & 9

Courage: The Defining Quality of Great Leaders

Martin Luther King Jr.
'The ultimate measure of a man is not where he stands in moments of comfort, but where he stands at times of challenge and controversy'

Courage or bravery is the quality of spirit and conduct that enables a person to face difficulty, challenges, danger, and pain without fear. It takes courage to stand up for what is right. It takes selfless courage to stand against evil in any society and the nation, to deal with corruption and establish righteousness. To act in accordance with one's convictions, especially in the face of criticism you need to be courageous not to compromise on your convictions, values and well tested principles of righteousness and justice. Talk is cheap, it takes courage to be proactively committed and consistently dedicated to building the future we want to see in our marriages, workplaces, marketplaces, communities, politics and government, to establish good governance in our society at large.

It takes courage to lead and raise the banner of righteousness in any society. To fulfil your God-given vision, purpose, mandate and assignment on the thrones and any leadership position, you need to be courageous. You need to be courageous enough to defeat your fears because courage is not the absence of fear, but the triumph over fear. Leadership takes making bold, often unpopular decisions and without this leadership quality you will be practically dysfunctional to operate on the thrones and any leadership position.

Within the last twenty-six years, we have worked with and mentored many traditional leaders, marketplace leaders and key political office holders. I have found out that courage is key defining quality of leaders to take bold initiatives to transform their communities and the society, courage to challenge the status quo, to take unpopular decisions with potential for revolutionary change, good governance and transformation in their domains. The throne and any position of leadership is a place of challenges and controversies, so courage is at the core and foundation of what it takes to lead and to operate on thrones. All leaders need courage to create sustainable success.

Why is Courage So Important?

In leadership and the operational dynamics of thrones, you will always have issues that threatens you or a purpose and assignment that overwhelms you. You will always have to take decisions or act in a way that corresponds to risk appropriately, not over-confidently or in a cowardly way to accomplish good things and fulfil the assignment of the throne. Courage separates effective leaders from ineffective leaders and counts as one of the foundations of great leadership.

Courage enhances influence through trust when you are honest and brave enough to be honest with yourself and with others, it builds accountability whereby people are not afraid to hold each other accountable because it is the right thing to do, it builds and grows our capacity to resolve conflicts whereby we are not afraid to speak up and challenge others, critic ideas and take responsibility to engage in creative and productive conflict to solve problems. Without courage you cannot make a difference. Other qualities such as integrity, honesty, making decisions and communication skills are qualities of a good leader, but all these require courage for full expression. Courageous leadership must start from within the leader's heart. It is the place where courage resides.

Elements of Courage

1. Courageous people are people who know who they are and what they stand for because knowing who you are, your identity is a solid ground on which to stand. One of the greatest barriers to courage is not knowing who you are. Knowing who am I and what God has called me to do is at the root of my courage acts and decisions.
2. Courageous people are purposeful. They know their purpose in life and pursue it tenaciously. It is said that if the purpose of a thing is not known, abuse is inevitable.
3. Courageous people are passionate about their beliefs, purpose and values in life. The inspired word of God in Hebrews 12:1-3, teaches us that the key to persistence is passion and being zealous about one's purpose.
4. Staying the Course – No matter how tough it is, courageous people stay the course patiently. Courageous people are resilient, can maintain control over a situation and think of new ways to solve a problem, but they don't give up trying. They always find a way to bounce back if they do not succeed in a course of action.
5. Taking risks – Not foolish but calculated and necessary aimed at moving things forward. Sometimes to achieve a purpose requires the courage to face the fear of the unknown or a measure of uncertainty.
6. Courageous people take action – Another element of courage is willingness to initiate and take action. Leaders do not wait for

somebody to do something before they take action. They are willing to take bold initiatives.

7. Courageous leaders lead and operate on the thrones with principles that guide them when pressure mounts and when they are faced with challenges.

What Enhances the Leadership Quality of Courage?

1. The fear of the Lord – the fear of the LORD brings strong confidence and courage this is the key to establish justice on the throne. A leadership established in the fear of God is a fountain of life.
2. Integrity of heart – Courage is the ability to do what needs to be done, regardless of the risk. Integrity is the ability to do what is right. A leader who can consistently do the right things, when they need to be done, is a leader with courage
3. Skilfulness of hands – skilfulness and competence bring confidence and courage
4. Living purposefully – when you are focused on your purpose and the joy set before you, you are emboldened in your pursuit. "...*For the joy set before him, he endured the cross, scorning its shame..,*" Hebrews 12:2
5. Being prepared and ready to die for your vision and values. A leader with courage is a leader who believes that a vision worth living for is a vision worth dying for at the same time.

Why Do Some Leaders Lack the Courage to Operate on the Thrones Successfully?

1. Fear of men and not the fear of God – the fear of men ensnares leaders, but the fear of God enhances courage. When you fear men, you will lose courage most of the time.
2. No proper training. Leading is a great and challenging task that requires proper training and mentorship. Preparation for leadership is key to success.
3. Heart not prepared for throne assignment. You must put your

heart where your vision is and when the heart is not adequately prepared to do what is right, the end could be disastrous.

4. Incompetence and mediocrity. Competency and skillfulness produce courage and incompetence will make you lose confidence in yourself.

What are the Types of Courage?

Physical Courage

Physical courage is a display of bravery when faced with physical danger, hardship, and threat to death or even death. A good example is what we see when a firefighter goes into a burning building to save lives or when divers dive into deep sea to save lives. Other examples are facing an enemy on the battlefield as David faced Goliath in the battle or even when climbing a mountain. Queen Esther is a good example and profile of physical courage. Haman, the king's adviser had plotted to destroy all the Jews in the land.

Esther, the queen was asked by her cousin Mordecai to go to the king and ask him to save her people, the Jews. However, approaching the king without an invitation was a crime punishable by death in Persia kingdom unless the king raised his sceptre of approval. Nevertheless, Esther rose up to the challenge, a demonstration of exceptional courage and risked her life to save the Jews from being annihilated. Esther decided to go unto the king which is not according to the law and declared: ***"if I perish, I perish"*** (Esther 4:16). She obtained the king's favour and eventually used her position and influence to save her people.

Social Courage

Social behavioural courage is the quality or virtue of being able to express your thoughts or opinions, and willingness to demonstrate your true self even if it means risking social disapproval, criticism or condemnation. It is a state of mind or composure whereby you are comfortable in your own space and not conforming to the expectations of others, yet you are also willing to let others be themselves in your heart.

Moses is a wonderful example of social courage in his challenge to

Pharaoh and the Egyptian establishment. Particularly given his initial timidity and hesitation. He first had to face Pharaoh – the leader of the most powerful nation on earth at that time. When God called him to lead, he tried to come up with excuses so that he would not have to do it. He saw himself as being unsuitable to stand up to Pharaoh (Exodus 3:11). He was afraid that the Israelites would not listen to him (Exodus 4:1). Nevertheless, he faced his insecurities and fears, stood against Pharaoh, and led the people out of bondage.

Moral Courage

This is the trait or virtue of the willingness to speak out and take action to do what is right even in the face of opposition. It is the fortitude or strength of character to do the right thing even if it is not popular. Moral courage is the display of fundamental virtues of honesty, fidelity, respect, fairness, integrity and taking responsibility. Moral courage enables us to rise above hatred, socio-cultural divisions, apathy and complacency in our political divides and religious differences. Nelson Mandela comes to mind as a great example of moral courage, who through moral courage navigated the dark historical legacy of South Africa and unified racially segregated people.

In 1 Samuel 30, David displayed phenomenal moral courage when he declared an important principle that those who went with him to battle and defeated the Amalekites and those of his men who were too weak to pursue the Amalekites should receive an equal portion of the spoils despite the objection and protest by some of his men who went with him to the battle.

Spiritual Courage

Spiritual courage is essentially the quality of character that is stimulated by faith in God, His word and the power of the Holy Spirit to take on the mysteries of life, our purpose here on earth and to establish the kingdom of God. It is the courage to believe in the truth of God and practice. When God commissioned Joshua, He commanded him, "Be strong and of a good courage..." (Joshua 1:6-7). Joshua demonstrated spiritual courage to lead the nation of Israel to the Promised Land.

This is also the courage to forgive and to love. Society is fragmented by walls of hatred, greed, selfishness and ethnicity. Many leaders lack the spiritual courage to operate on the thrones because thrones are spiritual and it takes a man or woman who is spiritually courageous in the power of love and forgiveness to operate on thrones. Joshua demonstrated courage to forgive the Gibeonites who tricked them into a covenant. The Gibeonites asked Joshua and the leaders of Israel to make a treaty with them and promise to protect them. Joshua did not ask the Lord's counsel but simply agreed to the treaty. When the Israelites discovered that they had been deceived, yet they knew they had to keep the promise in the spirit of forgiveness.

Again, David's encounter with Goliath is another demonstration of spiritual courage, especially when his orientation on hearing the taunts of the giant is compared to the fear that paralyzed the entire Israelite army.

Where Does Spiritual Courage to Operate on the Thrones Come From?

The major source of courage is the inspired word of God, the Book of the Law.

The Book of the Law

This Book of the Law shall not depart from your mouth, but you shall meditate in it day and night, that you may observe to do according to all that is written in it. For then you will make your way prosperous, and then you will have good success. Joshua 1:8

Dealing with the Spirit of Discouragement

King David encouraged himself in the Lord -1 Samuel 30:6.

David Encouraged Himself in the Lord

Now David was greatly distressed, for the people spoke of stoning him, because the soul of all the people was grieved, every man for his sons and his daughters. But David strengthened himself in the Lord his God. – 1 Samuel 30:6.

Anyone who must operate successfully on the thrones must learn to deal with discouragement because discouragement is one of the most lethal weapons of the enemy to attack and sap our courage.

1. You must understand and acknowledge that there is a spirit called discouragement and that no one is immune against the attack of discouragement so you need to be on the watch. No matter who you are, we all go through times of discouragement.
2. You must understand too that discouragement is subtle and comes when least expected especially at the height of a successful venture.
3. No matter what happens, be yourself. Nothing is more discouraging than trying to be something you are not.
4. Stop comparing yourself or marriage with others, rather commit yourself to gratitude and to improving yourself and your skills.
5. Take time for rest and renewal. No matter what height you reach in life, you will always be discouraged when you don't take time for rest and renewal.
6. Watch and Pray.
7. Believe in your vision and understand that a vision worth living for is also worth dying for.

How to Develop the Leadership Qualities of Courage

Courage is a skill: The good news is that everyone has the capacity for being courageous and courage is a teachable and learnable skill. Never underestimate yourself. Therefore, it is heart-warming and interesting that the leadership qualities of courage can be developed. It is not something you are born with, but something you can learn. Developing the habit and culture of Courage requires clear purpose, self-awareness, managing emotions of fear, willingness to stick your neck out of your comfort zone, intentional and consistent practice of taking bold initiatives among other things:

1. Develop a clear purpose statement and focus on your purpose. Building courage starts with clarity of purpose and commitment to it. Clarity produces power, a life without a clear purpose statement lack direction, focus and cannot fuel courage. *"**For this I was born, and for this I came into the world, to bear witness to**

the truth,... " John 18:37

2. Self-awareness: understand and be comfortable with who you are. Know your strengths and weaknesses
3. Confront and manage your emotions of fear: identify your fears and challenges, acknowledge them and confront them. Remember, courage is not the absence of fear but ability to act despite fear
4. Develop strong ethical values: Be driven by strong values of Godliness, integrity, truth, honesty, righteousness, justice and ability to live above instant gratifications.
5. Mentorship: I favour mentorship any day. Be accountable to mentors who can provide counsels and encouragement.
6. Take responsibility for your actions: be willing to admit and learn from your mistakes and be transparent. Authenticity inspires trust and boldness
7. Do not be afraid of moving out of your comfort zone: set clear goals and take on new initiatives. Experience they say, is the best teacher.

18.

DEALING WITH THE THRONES OF INIQUITY

Thrones are Created by God and for God

Thrones are created by God and we need to teach men and women to understand God's perspective of thrones, because the Christian theology of government and thrones is faulty and the enemy has taken advantage of this for a long time. All believers are to be seated on the thrones – the seat of authority and governing power, but not so in most cases because of lack of knowledge. We need to understand the implications that thrones are created by God and for God so that in all things He may have pre-eminence.

Colossians 1:16-18

For by Him all things were created that are in heaven and that are on earth, visible and invisible, whether thrones or dominions or principalities or powers. All things were created through Him and for Him. And He is before all things, and in Him all things consist. And He is the head of the body, the church, who is the beginning, the firstborn from the dead, that in all things He may have the pre-eminence.

God made thrones visible and invisible. Some thrones are visible: kings rule territories and domains with authority. However, some thrones and powers are not visible even though they are very real, but you cannot see them with your natural eyes. God seats on His Throne in heaven even though you cannot see the Throne with the natural eye, but He rules in the affairs of the universe. This is one foundational quality of faith which is a firm conviction about the invisible, non-tangible realities. By faith we understand that God created the world out of nothing which is attested to in Hebrews 11:3:

"By faith we understand that the worlds were framed by the word of God, so that the things which are seen were not made of things which are visible".

The invisible satanic thrones battles to govern the visible thrones on the earth in order to establish corrupt, wicked, demonic culture and ideologies on the earth when the earthly kings or leaders enter into covenants with the kingdom of darkness and surrender the thrones to Satan and demons of darkness. This is the special feature of the church at Pergamos (Revelation 2:12-17), a city where Satan had his throne. The battle is always who is going to seat on the throne. It is about who controls the thrones both the physical and in the spirit realm – visible and invisible. To capture or significantly influence a territory or a region you must first of all capture the throne, the seat of authority and seat of governing power, visible and invisible.

The Thrones of Iniquity

God sets up thrones of righteousness to advance His counsel on earth, however we need to know that Satan sets up thrones of iniquity as a strategic measure to frustrate, delay and thwart the will of God. It is a deliberate and calculated effort to oppose the counsel of God on earth. The reason for this is the fact that thrones are extremely influential and effective in the organization of human affairs. We need to understanding and identify the thrones of iniquity that are ruling and influencing the thrones on the earth. The throne of iniquity is figuratively used to describe positions of power, authority and thrones characterised by evil, corruption and wicked practices.

It means wickedness in high places, wickedness enthroned upon the seat of judgment, a description of corrupt, tyrannical government where Satan is the king ruling through earthly kings or leaders through invisible satanic thrones. There are thrones of iniquity that we must destroy and overthrow in most communities and nations in order to usher in righteous governance. However, to overthrow the thrones of iniquity poses a great challenge in every nation, but it is very crucial in order to establish the throne of righteousness in certain situations. No doubt, we need the help of the Spirit of God to deal with corrupt culture and wicked thrones of iniquity that produces bad leadership.

What is Iniquity?

Iniquity – a repeated violation of the right or duty that mankind is under obligation to do, wicked act, immoral conduct or practice. Iniquity means calamity, destruction, ruin, or disaster. It also refer to the trouble itself (Psalm 19:13), or to the cause of the calamity which is wickedness (Psalm 5:9).

Psalm 94:20, 21

Shall the throne of iniquity, which devises evil by law, Have fellowship with You? They gather together against the life of the righteous, And condemn innocent blood. But the Lord has been my defense, And my God the rock of my refuge. He has brought on them their own iniquity, And shall cut them off in their own wickedness; The Lord our God shall cut them off.

The psalmist in the text above gave a vivid description of thrones of iniquity. By taking a diligent look, we can learn the characteristics and features of the thrones of iniquity and gain important principles on how to confront thrones of iniquity in our communities and nations. Thrones of iniquity is when iniquity is established in high places, wickedness enthroned upon seat of judgements, delivering unjust sentences. The thrones or civil authority that brings ruin, calamity, disaster on a people because of the wickedness of the rulers and their advisers. Thrones of iniquity are a deliberate design of the enemy. Psalm 1:1 lays out the structural make-up of the kingdom of darkness. There is a counsel or philosophy, a way and a seat of the ungodly which speaks of high positions and thrones dedicated to wickedness.

Characteristics of Thrones of Iniquity

- **Frames Mischief by Law**

Frames denotes the action of devising, forming, fashioning, or planning which indicates that the activity of devising is continuous. These wicked rulers continually devise or plan "mischief by a statute." It is their habitual practice. The term 'mischief' indicates any grievance, misery, perverseness, pain or sorrow. The throne of iniquity devises trouble and grief by means of legal decrees. These thrones, kings or rulers use their authority to frame laws that bring misery and sorrow to the people they govern. This means of course that mere legality is not righteousness. Just because something is legal, traditional or cultural does not equate to righteousness. There are not a few practices that readily answer to the definition of iniquity which wears the cloak of legality.

- **Gather Together Against the Life of The Righteous.**

Thrones of iniquity 'gather themselves against the soul of the righteous.' This indicates that they persecute the people of God, those who worship God and walk in obedience to His law; who seek to lead a peaceable life in the land and of course those who speaks against their practices and evils. One reliable feature of a throne of iniquity is that it is predatory and antagonistic toward the righteous. King Jeroboam chased away the priests and Levites from Israel. King Ahab and Jezebel specialized in murdering prophets of God.

- **Condemn Innocent Blood.**

To condemn innocent blood is to declare the guiltless guilty, to punish them for a crime they did not commit. The book of Proverbs describes such injustice as an abomination:

Proverbs 17:15 KJV
He that justifieth the wicked, and he that condemneth the just,
even both are an abomination to the Lord.

To condemn innocent blood also involves oppressing and destroying the lives of less privilege in the society as stated in Psalms 94:6, where the conduct of the throne of iniquity against the weak is described as follows:

"They slay the widow and the stranger, and murder the fatherless."

Bloodshed of innocents is always a feature of thrones of iniquity.

Key Features of the Thrones of Iniquity:

- Thrones that kill God's servants and the righteous.
- Thrones that destroy the royal seeds.
- Thrones that disrupt and destroys destinies of people and nations.
- Thrones that justify the wicked, but condemns the just.
- Thrones that condemn innocent blood.
- Thrones that oppress the weak, the poor, the helpless and murders the fatherless.
- Thrones that slay the widow and the stranger.
- Thrones that oppose the purpose of God.
- Thrones of iniquity exhibits corruption, evils and wickedness continually.

Overthrowing the Thrones of Iniquity

In Psalm 94, the psalmist pleaded with God to rise up in judgment against the wicked rulers and throne, to establish righteousness in the seats of power.

1. Firstly, we need to understand that dealing with thrones of iniquity is a function of divine judgment. The way Jehu dealt with the house of Ahab is instructive (2 Kings 10) as well as the way Jehoiada, the priest dealt with Attaliah (2 Kings 11).
2. Secondly, we must bear it in mind that challenging corruption or injustice and the thrones of iniquity can be a long and arduous task and process. Patience, perseverance, and a commitment to righteousness and justice are crucial.
3. Moreover, before you can deal with thrones of iniquity in the land, you need to deal with iniquity in your heart, the desperate wickedness in your heart.

Psalm 66:18-20
If I regard iniquity in my heart, the Lord will not hear me:
But verily God hath heard me; he hath attended to the voice of
my prayer.

Blessed be God, which hath not turned away my prayer, nor his mercy from me.

You need to pray earnestly that iniquity will not prevail against you – Psalm 65:1-3.

4. We need to know that God does overthrow the thrones of wickedness and we have to cooperate with Him in this purpose with clarity and understanding

"The wicked are overthrown, and are not; but the house of the righteous shall stand" (Proverbs 12:7).
"The house of the wicked shall be overthrown: but the tabernacle of the upright shall flourish" (Proverbs 14:11).

5. We need to develop corporate strategy and unity of purpose in our communities and nations in order to overthrow the thrones of wickedness. This is not a one-man affair, but a corporate warfare.
6. We need high-level prayers that will activate the release of angels – the Sabaoth in order to overthrow thrones of wickedness in any territory.
7. This one can be established by prayers with fastings.

Prayers to Overthrow the Wicked – Psalm 10

19.

REDEEMING THE THRONES – DEALING WITH FOUNDATIONS

The king and the throne are two powerful entities, and the king's influence, authority and power are determined by the throne upon which they sit. However, every throne has its own peculiarity, carries its own unique identity, and exhibits its own characteristics and nature that impacts the life of the person who sit on it. When a good king is enthroned on a perverted throne, he may end up becoming a wicked ruler.

This is one of the mysteries of the thrones that we need to understand which will help us to comprehend why many kings, even Godly kings and leaders struggle to do what is right on the thrones and finish well. With this understanding, we need to be proactive in training leaders and dealing with foundations of thrones that makes leaders to struggle with transforming their domains. Again, as a king may be guilty of sins to the detriment of the nation, so also the thrones as may be adjured guilty based on what present or past king has done while on the throne. This always have serious consequences for the land and the people:

And the woman of Tekoah said unto the king, My lord, O king, the iniquity be on me, and on my father's house: and the king and his throne be guiltless. *2 Samuel 14:9*

Moreover, thrones have foundations and these foundations affects the person who sits on the throne positively or negatively depending on the nature of the foundation of the throne; good or bad, Godly or occultic. It does not matter if a righteous person sit on the throne, the foundations of thrones must be addressed effectively. Thrones must be redeemed in order for kings and people in authority to effectively accomplish the thrones assignment and transform the nation.

Before we can establish thrones of righteousness and justice in the land, there is a need to address the iniquities and foundations of thrones, redeem the thrones from perverse and occult foundations, and dedicate the throne to God in order for the king and the throne to function with capacity for righteousness and justice. This initiative of redeeming thrones in order to redeem the land and release nations into their redemptive purposes must include practical strategies of cleansing the thrones as part of the throne paradigm towards good governance among the nations.

The cleansing of thrones, the breaking of traditional occult bondages on the thrones of nations must be understood as a key step in the process of step by step, throne by throne, kingdom by kingdom, releasing the nations out of foundations of thrones that produces wicked rulers and bad leadership, and dealing with foundations that promotes satanic policies against God's principles and purposes amongst the nations.

Even in certain cases, where ancient thrones and kingdoms no longer exist, where old, ancient thrones and royal houses were established before but no longer exist, the occult bondages may still be in place constituting a major blockage of the redemption of the land, the resources of the people, and the purposes of God. Therefore, there must be diligent research into the history of the thrones, adequate spiritual mapping and thorough cleansing of such ancient thrones and gates in the land. This practical process is part of the initiatives of The Global Throne Movement which is explained further in the last chapter of this book.

The Seat of Government

People tend to wonder when people in government take certain decisions, wondering if something is wrong with the thinking process at the highest level of governance, but the truth is that when people at the seat of power or government make mistakes, they are most likely victims of a force higher than we can imagine emanating from the foundations of the thrones. When someone get to the seat of government, if such does not know how to deal with foundations of thrones, they may act like they are under a spell. Some mistakes made by kings, leaders of organisations and government do not look normal at times.

There are so many dynamics, structures, powers and spiritual dimensions that surrounds the thrones of the government of nations in particular that show that the seat of government as an entity need redemption. Leaders make wrong decisions when there is a cloud of darkness or evil powers around them. Dedicating the seat of government to the Almighty King of kings is very crucial to subdue invisible thrones, powers and principalities that contend against the leaders and the throne.

Foundations of thrones

Thrones have foundations which influence whoever sit on it. Understanding and dealing with the foundations of thrones is a specialised training that people must acquire in order to function effectively as kings and other places of authority to be able to bring genuine and sustainable transformation and righteous governance. Take the case of the foundation laid by Jeroboam, the son of Nebat, who taught Israel to sin. Jeroboam started well; however he developed a desperate desire to secure himself on the throne through the introduction of foundational, territorial and systemic idolatry; rather he plunged the entire nation into iniquity which had negative influence on subsequent kings that ruled after him.

The Bible stated that he did more evil than all who lived before him: only a few of the kings that ruled after him, the Bible records, did what was good in the sight of God, but they never departed from the sins of Jeroboam, the son of Nebat (2 kings 3:3; 10:29). King Jeroboam became the benchmark of iniquity and perversion on the throne and when we look at certain nations of the world, there are leaders with benchmark of iniquity that their evil foundations are still affecting the leadership structure of their nations.

Foundations of God's Throne

God has a throne and His Throne is established forever and ever; the sceptre of righteousness is the sceptre of His Throne (Psalm 40: 6-7). Revelation 4 describes the awesomeness of the Throne of God, the nature of the Throne and the things that proceed from the Throne. God's Throne has foundations. Psalm 89:14 and Psalm 97:2 describes the foundation of God's throne:

Justice and judgment are the habitation of thy throne: mercy and truth shall go before thy face.
Blessed is the people that know the joyful sound: they shall walk, O Lord, in the light of thy countenance.
In thy name shall they rejoice all the day: and in thy righteousness shall they be exalted. Psalm 89:14-16

The LORD reigns; Let the earth rejoice; Let the multitude of isle be glad. Clouds and darkness are round about him: righteousness and judgment are the habitation of his throne. Psalm 97:1, 2

These two, Righteousness and Justice, are the foundation of God's throne. The nature of the foundations of God's Throne exhibits and manifests righteousness and justice, mercy and truth goes before His Throne. This is the only template for thrones to reign in righteousness. Foundations of thrones everywhere must be patterned and laid on this template and principle.

Foundations of Earthly Thrones

It is God's plan that every earthly throne will be connected and be an extension of His Throne in order for the throne to prosper and to establish His purposes here on earth. For, all thrones belong to God.

Then Solomon sat on the throne of the Lord as king instead of David his father, and prospered; and all Israel obeyed him.
And all the princes, and the mighty men, and all the sons likewise of king David, submitted themselves unto Solomon the king.
And the Lord magnified Solomon exceedingly in the sight of all Israel, and bestowed upon him such royal majesty as had not been on any king before him in Israel. 1 Chronicles 29:23-25

Therefore, God expects each throne to be founded on righteousness and justice, unfortunately, this is not so in most cases. Most of the earthly thrones have strong foundations of idolatry, bloodshed, sorcery, occultism, witchcraft, slavery and wickedness. These foundations affect and influence those who sit on them as well as the land and the people in one way or another.

Manifestations of Faulty or Wicked Foundations of Thrones

Below are some of the manifestations of wrong and faulty foundations of most earthly thrones when they are not properly cleansed and redeemed:

- These foundations make kings to be disconnected from God and to oppose God like Pharaoh did instead to establish God's purposes for the thrones.
- These foundations make it difficult for kings to serve the living God with a perfect heart most of the time, even if in their heart they secretly love God.
- These foundations make demands for blood at times even human blood, especially when a king dies or when a new king is to be installed.
- These foundations also cause bloodshed through kingship and chieftaincy tussles. There are communities that have not known peace till date due to chieftaincy tussles even amongst the same kith and kin.
- These foundations ensnare the kings themselves because it brings them under terrible fear and taboos. A king must not have only one wife. He must not see his mother and or his first son any more after his installation. These are some of the demands emanating from occultic and faulty throne foundations that make kings to live in perpetual bondage and make them a shadow of themselves.
- These foundations make kings to be lonely and miserable. A brother shared with me how they visited a king in a big palace. Right from the entrance to the place where they met the king, there was nobody save two fowls fighting. They shouted to announce their coming, nobody answered. When they eventually got to where he was, the king was sleeping on a chair. They greeted him casually and told him they wanted to see the king. The king retorted: "Don't I look like one?" With fear and haste they quickly greeted him. Then they shared the gospel and prayed with

him. As they were about to leave, the King told them that he was usually alone, and asked why were they leaving him so soon'? A lot of kings find themselves in situations where they really need the help of God and believers who know how to deal with thrones.

- In some communities, because of these foundations they insist that some kings must see certain voodoo priests as their last visitors before going to bed and/or the first guests in the morning. What do you expect from that type of arrangement?
- These foundations make it impossible for kings to reign in righteousness and administer justice. A lot of the foundations are sown in wickedness. These foundations make it difficult, if not impossible for kings to depart from evil.
- These foundations empower the kings with a great level of satanic spiritual powers that makes them to rule their people with a fist of iron and wickedness.
- These foundations make some kings to oppose the gospel especially when you begin to deal with the issues of idolatry and festivals in their domain because they are the custodians of the people's idols, the traditions, customs and cultures of the land.
- These foundations speak, and make the whole land to fight against any king who renounces the idols of the land, sometimes.

Other Parameters of the Foundations of Earthly Thrones

Here, we will consider other specific things or factors that go with the foundations of earthly thrones in most communities and nations:

Installation/Enthronement/Coronation Rites

The rites are the fundamental acts (or sets of rituals) performed according to the customs and traditions of the land or as dictated by oracles. During the process of installation or enthronement, kings are usually put in confinement for certain days, weeks and months. Various rituals and sacrifices will be going on. The king will be taken to different strong altars and locations in the land at night such as the graveyard of past kings, the marketplaces and other dedicated sacred places. It is believed that kings and leaders must not come out as ordinary men but, be fully fortified with strong powers and transformed into a demigod.

In one community, I was informed the king must bathe himself standing upon a naked human being and thereafter break a coconut on the head of the unlucky man. In another community, the king must have sexual intercourse with a woman and afterwards, both the king and the woman must never see eye to eye again. In a certain community, the king will be paraded around the community, the people will be raining curses on the king and vice versa. These are some of the issues we have encountered and dealt with in many communities with their kings and thrones by God's grace and mercy before those communities were released into prosperity and their redemptive purposes.

Initiation

Kings and leaders in many cases are usually initiated into all the secret and occult societies in the land before they could be coronated. They enter a covenant with the unrighteous men in the land and by implication they are no longer able to speak against evil men and women; with the consequence that righteousness is denied in the land.

Past Kings

Kings are usually deified after death especially the first king of the land, and usually, they invoke their spirits upon the throne when a new king is to be installed. Sins of past kings become a foundation inherited by the new one and if these sins are not properly atoned for, it will continue to affect the throne, the king, and the people of the land. There was a famine during David's reign that lasted for three years, even though David was a man after God's heart:

Now there was a famine in the days of David for three years, year after year; and David inquired of the Lord. And the Lord answered, "It is because of Saul and his [a]bloodthirsty house, because he killed the Gibeonites."
So the king called the Gibeonites and spoke to them. Now the Gibeonites were not of the children of Israel, but of the remnant of the Amorites; the children of Israel had sworn protection to them, but Saul had sought to kill them in his zeal for the children of Israel and Judah.
Therefore, David said to the Gibeonites, "What shall I do for you?

Here, we observed that King David had to make atonement for the iniquity of King Saul, his predecessor before the famine of three years could be averted. The sin of a king is not a personal sin, but a national sin. In redeeming the thrones, we must research into the history of all the past kings; what happened when they were on the throne.

Traditional Titles

Many traditional kings and leaders for example, take traditional titles. Some of these titles are either inherited or brought forth through divination during their installation. The titles have deep implications concerning the king and the throne. These titles in many cases invoke some satanic powers and anointing. Some of the titles could provoke God to jealousy. For example, a king or a leader taking the title of King of kings or the owner of the whole earth.

Calabash Opening Ceremony

It is required as part of the rites for the king to "open one out of many calabashes" prepared for him by the priests of idols in the land. They will tie a cloth on the face of the king so that he cannot see and ask him to proceed and carry one of the calabashes while they will be beating traditional drums. It is the belief of the people according to tradition that whichever calabash the new king opens will determine what will happen during his reign. If he opens a calabash containing a sword, then there would be wars during his reign. If he opens one containing red palm-kernel, it means there would be diseases during his tenure, or another containing ashes, which presupposes poverty and diseases during his reign. When these things begin to happen in the communities, people will be dealing with the problems, but the cause is hidden from them which is from the foundation of the thrones.

Totems

A totem is a natural object or animal that is believed by a particular group of people to have spiritual significance and that is adopted by it as an emblem, praise name or sacred object of worship which carries a special spiritual connection with a particular throne or tribe. Different types of totems are attached to the thrones in many cases to give the king added demonic powers and protection. Egyptian Pharaohs wore a totem of snakes on their crown. Some carry images of crocodiles; others wear skins of carnivorous animals. These may lead to the person sitting on the throne being possessed by these things and provoked to do wickedly in accordance with the behaviour of the wild beast whose image they adopt and are obliged to wear.

Dedicated Crowns

In many cases, the crowns of kings are usually dedicated to satanic powers before the king could be crowned. There are ancient crowns that are being worshipped as deities in some palaces. These crowns are not worn by the kings anyhow; it must not even be brought out without blood sacrifice. Some of them are worn once a year, or once in seven years. Some, when the king wears them, he must not see his own shadow.

The Seat or Stool

The seat or the stool is the throne upon which the king sits. Apart from the king himself, in most cases, the seats or stool of kings are strongly dedicated before the kings can sit upon them. If you get to the palace of certain kings, merely looking at the throne and the things paraded around the throne will inform you that whoever must sit upon such a throne cannot be ordinary.

Burial Rites

In many parts of the world, kings and leaders are not buried as ordinary men. There are certain burial rites for kings depending on the culture, the traditions of the people and the foundation of the throne. In some cultures, there are rituals that the firstborn only must carry out before the king can be buried. The rites of passage of kings and natural rulers differ from kingdom to kingdom. In some communities, in the dark ages, kings are not buried without human sacrifices. It is part of the customs and traditions that a king must not die alone, so human beings must be buried alive. In fact, in a particular city, there is a chieftaincy title whose holder must die along with the king. In some parts, it is believed that the king cannot die but, he will transit to another world, they usually bury slaves alive with the king so that they can continue to serve him wherever the king has transited to. These days, the traditions are no more carried out, however, the effects of those practices live on. Where these abominable practices have taken place before; it is crucial that a proper and diligent cleansing process is carried out on the thrones.

Redeeming the Thrones

Despite all the evils embedded in the foundations of thrones, it is our strategic position that earthly thrones can be redeemed from all forms of evil, faulty and satanic foundations. Here we will consider some basic strategies we need to redeem the thrones of our communities and the seat of government. The fact that Jesus was crowned with thorns as King of kings, I believe, has laid for us a foundation for the redemption of the earthly thrones and the seat of government so that we can witness the reign of righteousness, justice and good governance.

Some Basic and Useful Strategies:

- Investigate properly the history of the throne and all the past kings, the names of the past kings, titles and what they did while on the throne.
- Take time to seek the face of God and receive strategies from God. Ask God to reveal hidden things about the throne and uncover the foundations of the throne to you.
- In redeeming a particular throne, you need to go as a group and you may need to stay in the palace for three days with fasting, seeking the face of God. In this case, a whole day may be dedicated to issues of repentance alone for far-reaching results.
- Lead the king into proper confessions and repentance of his sins, and that of the past kings one after another and do each one diligently. Do not be in a hurry. The sins of idolatry, occultism, bloodshed, slavery, wickedness, and all other sins must be properly and diligently atoned for.
- Let the king renounce all covenants that have been made upon the throne by himself and his predecessors.
- Deal with all the past dedications of the king and the thrones to satanic powers.

- Deal with the covenant of death over the throne. Isaiah 28:16.
- Deal with every element of the thrones. Pray over the crowns, ancient and modern, and the sceptre etc.
- Lay the foundations of the throne with the word of God. Psalm 138:4, Psalm 89:14, Isaiah 32:1-2.
- Let the king make a covenant with God upon the throne to connect his throne with the throne of God and to serve God with a perfect heart all the days.
- Let him declare that his throne has become the throne of Jesus Christ.
- Make a decree that no king will reign on the throne again who will not do the will of God. Pray for the king from Isaiah 11:1 for the seven Spirit of God to operate on the throne and anoint him sitting upon the throne.

God Is at Work

God is at work touching kings, their thrones and the seat of government in these last days. Traditional kings in Nigeria and Africa for instance are not just embracing the gospel, but they are also forsaking the idols of the land; and some are evangelists on the throne. We have today in Nigeria a Fellowship of Christian Traditional Rulers (FECTRON). We have in this fellowship, kings who were Christians before ascending their thrones and have not compromised their faith. Again, we also have among them those who were already kings and had passed through the traditional rites; but now, after experiencing salvation, have since turned away from worshipping idols and no longer participate in satanic festivals. Many are extending their hands of fellowship, asking to be assisted and helped to redeem their thrones and land. We pray that as God continues to help us, and His Spirit comes upon His people, all earthly thrones will bow to the Lordship of the true King of kings (Psalm 138:4, 5). Amen.

Prayer on the Foundations of the Thrones

- Thank God who sits upon His Throne in heaven and put kings upon thrones here on earth for His purposes. Proclaim Psalm 45:1-7.

- Identify with the sins of the king and repent over the wicked foundations of the throne since the inception of the throne.
- Deeply repent of the sins of past rulers/kings, and every wicked abomination ever committed on the throne, such as shedding of innocent blood, taking of other people's wives or land by force, etc.
- Repent of all the idolatrous festivals, and wicked abominable practices that provoke God to jealous.
- Surrender the thrones to God, to uncover every evil foundation and to uproot them.
- Turn over the throne to God and plead the blood of Jesus over the throne for total cleansing from evil dedications.
- Plead the blood of Jesus to speak better things concerning the throne. Instead of the blood crying for vengeance, let the blood of Jesus speak mercy over the throne.
- Ask God to uproot every evil speaking upon the throne that do not allow the throne to be established with righteousness and justice.
- Pray for grace and sincerity of heart for the king to stand against every fetish and occultic practices as king on the throne.
- Proclaim the Lordship of Jesus Christ upon the throne.

Testimony

A king was brought to my office for prayers. The battle to terminate his life was so much because he refused to worship the idols of the land. He suffered several attacks. He was sick to the point of death, yet the doctors diagnosed nothing. He had fasted many days according to him to deal with his problems. The more he fasted the more the attacks. Briefly, I explained to him the need to deal with his personal foundation and that of the throne he inherited. We ministered to him and life was restored to him. He said to me that he did not know he could survive the next day but God has kept him alive till date. Immediately he invited us to come and assist him to redeem his throne and the palace. He told us how he used to hear footsteps in and around his palace, particularly at night, but he would not see anybody no matter how much he searched. He experienced a series of terrible things like this.

In the palace, there was a room called "the king's strong room" where he could disappear at will, (perhaps as they say, to commune with the dead). In this room, there were no windows, no light, the walls, and ground were not plastered and nobody but, a king must enter it. The room contained the major altar in the palace. Since he became king, he had never entered the room even once and had not bothered himself about the room. After much prayers and times of seeking the face of God, I sent young men to the palace. The king was led into proper repentance and atonement for the ancestral sins of idolatry of the land was made through by the blood of Jesus. He was led to renounce all the covenants of the land with the idols; and to reject all the foundations that speak on the throne he inherited.

Then the young men entered the room and within two hours uprooted and brought out all the so-called gods and idolatrous articles and vessels one after the other. When the young men finished, the king himself set them on fire and said he would turn the room to either a library or prayer closet after renovation, to make the place more conforming to promote the grace of the Almighty God. Now, the king, his throne and the whole palace are dedicated to the true and the living God, and the community is enjoying unprecedented social and economic growth.

20.

THE KING'S ACADEMY: GROOMING DYNAMIC FUTURE LEADERS

Nebuchadnezzar, king of Babylon intentionally developed a strategic plan for raising, training and grooming the young talents he wanted to use to develop the intellectual, fiscal, administrative and economic institutions of his domain and nation. He targeted young, vibrant, royal elements among the captives. The king intentionally and strategically set in place an outcome-based training academy for three years to groom young people so that at the end of this period they might be well trained to serve the throne. He predetermined what they would eat and drink, and appointed trainers for them to produce people who would be able to serve him on the throne as palace administrators. The king instructed as to the qualifications, credentials of the young people to be trained:

- Youths without blemish.
- Well-favoured in appearance.
- Skillful in all wisdom.
- Skillful in discernment and understanding.
- Apt in learning knowledge.
- Competent to stand and serve in the king's palace.

From the school and the academy established by the King, we can learn the following:

- **Intentionality:** The king was intentional, deliberate and determined to pursue the goal of raising palace administrators – Isaiah 32.
- **Talents Hunt:** The king set up a process to find the best people for the throne assignments. He recruited and targeted gifted and talented young men of royal stock in his domain, they were not chosen because they were the king's relatives but rather by merit.

- **Outcome-based:** It was an outcome-based training academy with a clearly articulated idea of what the trainees are expected to know and be able to do, the skills and knowledge they must have.
- **Timelines:** Three year's timelines were scheduled to accomplish the task of the preparation of the trainees.
- **Throne Mindset:** The training was designed to reprogram their mindset to become palace personalities understanding the dynamics of thrones, government and governance.
- **Skills and Competence:** It was designed to build their character, competencies and capacity for their throne assignments.
- **Curriculum:** The curriculum was tailored towards the desired vision and goal. It appears we need to overhaul our training curriculum if we are to raise men and women who will have the capacity to deal with corrupt systems in our communities and nations.

To see the future we envisaged, we need to intentionally discern, raise, groom and mentor dynamic and spirited leaders to operate on the thrones. However, we need a better approach, curriculum and strategies to accomplish this goal.

What Should be the First Thing to Do to Prepare Kings/Officials for Their Throne Assignments?

Going by how King David mentored Solomon for the throne assignment, we understand that training and mentorship must be focused first and foremost on the integrity of heart and a loyal heart. The first tutorial handed down to Solomon was to serve God with a perfect heart and a willing mind, to understand that the LORD searches all heart and knows all the imaginations of the thoughts of the hearts – 1 Chronicle 28:9; 29:19.

What Type of Food?

Healthy eating and good health contribute to good brain development and function, sustained energy output, and being physically resilient. In a literal sense it is said that 'You Are What You Eat' which means it is important to eat good food that will promote good health and be able to perform optimally. Moreover, if you are given to too much food and strong drink, you can be sure you will ruin your throne assignment. A study of Daniel chapter one showed that Daniel acquired skills, wisdom and understanding ten times better than all the magicians and astrologers in the region because he purposed in his heart and did not defile himself with the portion of the king's meat nor with the wine. Daniel only ate vegetables and did not compromise on ritually unclean foods.

What Are The Qualities To Look For?

Borrowing a strategy from the king, we need to search for and train young people with the following credentials:

- Children without blemish
- Good looking morally and physically
- Gifted in all wisdom
- Possessing knowledge
- Quick to understand
- Teachable
- Able to choose good and reject evil

What Type of Training/Curriculum?

Outcome-based curriculum for kings and leaders must include the following fundamental and basic training among others:

- The integrity of heart and skillfulness of hands – Psalm 78:72
- The fear of God – Psalm 34:11, 2 Samuel 23:3
- Developing a strong sense of citizenship and national identity
- Developing a strong kingdom identity
- Understanding the fundamentals and dynamics of thrones
- Character Building – The development of character and maintaining the right perspective is at the heart of operating on the thrones because the challenges of the thrones and leadership will always reveal your character. Character-building is the training process of training and development to make someone emotionally stronger and better at dealing with problems and proffering solutions. Character traits define who you are and influences the choices you make in your life or your role as a leader especially at critical times. How a leader deals with circumstances

of life tells you many things about his character and values. Good character builds the foundation needed for sustainable success in life and helps people to perform their leadership roles effectively.

Can We Find Such a One as This?..... Genesis 41;38

Today, nations are plagued with a legion of men and women not fit to give wise counsel, yet our kings and leaders are often subjected to their wicked and deadly counsels. The dearth of good leaders is still the problem in many kingdoms and nations and the question about good governance in every domain is: **'Can we find such a one as this; a man in whom the Spirit of God is?'** Every domain needs people with wisdom to proffer solutions to the many-sided and complicated problems in the land and the nation. Joseph rose to power from the prison and patented the grain reserve technology to solve the problem of the greatest regional economy and most powerful nation of the time, as prime minister. He was able to reveal the king's dream, interpret the dream as well as implement a fourteen years' grain reserve strategies that saved the nation. Enough of rhetoric about problems and challenges, we need solutions and blueprints that will bring an end to corruption and bad leadership. We need solution-driven men and women with impeccable character to emerge as kings, leaders of nations and administrators in every domain of influence. But if we are not intentional, deliberate, proactive and strategic about raising such leaders now, your guess is as good as mine.

Conclusion

In conclusion, the highlights of how the type of intentional training discussed here sets thrones up for long-term development and success is evident in the lives of Daniel and his friends. Daniel and his friends were elevated to high positions in Babylon and at a time became the administrators of one hundred and twenty provinces. Daniel influenced the reigns of several kings. When Belshazzar was troubled with a dream and the whole of the kingdom with him, Daniel was summoned to proffer a solution and this is what was said by the queen concerning Daniel.

There is a Man in Thy Kingdom...*Daniel 5:11-14*

- In whom is the spirit of the Holy God
- Light, understanding and superior wisdom were found in him
- He had an excellent spirit, and knowledge and understanding
- He had the ability to interpret dreams
- He had the ability to clarify hard sentences
- Capacity to dissolve doubts
- Capacity to proffer solutions to knotty problems

Suffice to say these are the qualities of men and women that we need to raise and train for the thrones as kings, governors, administrators, ministers and leaders of nations. These are the qualities that can set up thrones for sustainable transformation, long-term development and success. This can be achieved through intentional, proactive preparation and outcome-based training discussed here.

21.

DEVELOPING PRODUCTIVE PLANS AND PROCESSES

God's Remnants and Hope for Communities (Jeremiah 23:3-8)

To establish a righteous reign and sustainable good governance in any society is not an easy task but, it is not an impossible one when there are people with the vision, right mindset, productive ideas, strong commitment, the dedication and who are willing to make the sacrifice that is required to oust oppressive and wicked government and kings in the land. Ousting wickedness and establishing righteousness is not a day's job or an exercise in wishful thinking. It is a process that requires adequate planning and careful implementation of strategies over time.

We will not wake up one day to see good governance without engaging with strategic and productive plans to establish processes that over time will usher in righteous people in places of authority and influence with good character, values, courage and capacity to effect positive change.

This calls for a lot of sacrifice and dedication to face opposition and challenges headlong. We need a remnant of men and women who are genuinely burdened for their locality or sphere of influence, a remnant who will discern, unveil, develop plans and strategies, confront, and prayerfully overthrow evil and wicked personalities that are in the position of power and have dominated governance; a remnant who will change systems, remove demonic ideologies and structures that destroy seed royals and oppress the people. We need a remnant that will develop capacities to deal with the reign of impunity in all domains of influence.

The Wicked Reign of Athaliah

Athaliah was the daughter of Ahab and Jezebel and the wife of Jehoram, king of Judah. After the death of Ahaziah, her son, Athaliah usurped the throne and reigned for six years. She killed all members of the royal house of Judah (2 Kings 11:1-3), except Joash. Her mother, Jezebel is the standard for usurping and manipulating thrones. The way she handled Ahab, executed state capture (wrote and sent letters in Ahab's name), arranged for Naboth to be defamed and killed by her nefarious network was a masterstroke.

The Preservation of the Heir to the Throne

Jehosheba the wife of Jehoiada the high priest, through her courage and quick-wittedness, was able to preserve Joash, an heir to the throne from the wicked sword of Athaliah. He was hidden in the house of the LORD for six years. The examples of Jehoiada and Jehosheba were primarily about strategic warfare and opposition against the enemies of good governance. It is therefore a template for the kind of spiritual and material warfare for thrones in order to bring an end to the reign of impunity and establish the reign of righteousness. Jehoiada established a successful process and organized actionable plans to oust Athaliah. She was killed and her wicked reign of bloodshed was brought to an end and a new righteous government was established in her place.

Athaliah and the Priest of Baal Are Representation Of:

- Mysterious and heartless personalities that destroy the royal heirs
- Powers of darkness that destroy the destinies of others they ought to protect
- Mysterious powers that enjoy manipulating and using the glory of others like kings Ahab and Saul
- Evil and mysterious powers, violent institutions and structures that thrive on shedding innocent blood
- Men and women operating from invisible wicked altars who have established demonic systems and raised up wicked and bad leaders for the nation
- Wicked personalities that deploy the powers of sorcery and witchcraft to manipulate, intimidate and oppress people in communities and nations like Elymas, the sorcerer in the Bible
- Wicked spirit of deception that deceives God's people to subvert God's purpose and good governance in order to carry out their wicked agenda

- Spiritual powers that instil fear over kingdoms, communities and nations through sorcery
- Evil powers that establish injustice, greed and corruption as a way of life and standard.

The Intervention of Jehoiada

Today, we are confronted with the fact that the governments of many nations and kingdoms are upon the wrong shoulders, greedy, wicked and bloody personalities. The issue now is how do we change this bedrock of evil and corruption? The practical intervention of Jehoiada, the priest brought an end to the wicked reign of Athaliah in his own time.

Are there ideas we can adopt from what was developed by Jehoiada to tackle evil and oppressive government today?

Jehoiada was a godly man who was concerned with restoring a righteous reign in the land. He developed productive and actionable plans, developed the political might of the priesthood and the house of God and set up a seven-year strategic plan to overthrow oppressive, wicked and bloody reign in the land. This to me is one of the missing links: just waking up during election cycles without establishing proper planning and strategies is a waste of time. You don't build good governance overnight. Of course, it takes a process and concerted and consistent efforts.

Implementation of Strategies that Ousted Wicked Reign

- Establishing strong priesthood everywhere with a unity of purpose – this is where we need to work very hard because in most nations there is a monumental disunity in the house of God. Building a network of men and women who understand this purpose of establishing righteousness in the land and are willing to pursue the mission.
- Developing the political might of the priesthood and raising territorial priests in each territory or domain of influence. This is done by creating awareness among godly men and women in the land, vision sharing and engagement with righteous people in the land for their buy-in process.

- Establishing a strong and righteous financial base for the process – resources from the house of God were used to establish the righteous. Everyone needs to see how they fit into the whole process. Importantly, there are righteous people to be mobilised for financial resources. The process is demanding financially and the resources must come from righteous men and women. The enemy has been using the power of financial control to scuttle the establishment of righteous government and now we need to develop a godly strategy for raising financial resources for a good cause.
- Courage and strong determination – uncommon audacity and fearlessness. Definitely, this is a process that requires the hands of men and women of courage to face challenges headlong.
- Productive plans, processes and strategies were outlined in a seven-year timeline. For six years most people believed all the heirs had been destroyed, that there was no legitimate heir to the throne to displace Attaliah. However, secretly Jehoaida was brainstorming with the remnants and planning and developing strategies to end impunity in the land. The planning went on for six years before the time of action. I favour this approach of putting heads together, brainstorming, and developing actionable plans with timelines over a period of time.
- Mobilizing people of like vision and mind. For a good cause, we need to network together. This is a great task that requires the gifts, skills and expertise of people with the burden for righteous government.
- Informed, strategic prayers and intercession. This process cannot be achieved except by prayers with fasting. We need to rebuild the altars of prayers in the community through reconciliation, repentance and forgiveness among the people of God.
- Understanding timing for action. Timing is very important in whatever we do. It took Jehoaida seven years of planning and execution. This is a process that can only be developed over a period of time and not a day.
- Discerning the peculiar adversaries of God's purpose on the thrones. There is a need to discern and analyse usurpers and opposing forces against righteousness in the land.
- Dealing with the foundations and thrones of iniquity in the land.

We need to identify the thrones of iniquity and wickedness in the land as well as a faulty foundation of thrones that produces bad and wicked leadership in the land. All these we have to deal with in prayers strategically. For instance, Athaliah was the daughter of Ahab and Jezebel, with an inheritance of dreadful lust and foundation to usurp power and manipulations.

- Enthroning righteous people on the thrones and government. We need to discern and identify the right people for the thrones. When the right people are not on the throne, the people suffer. In this example, everyone knew their position and was able to keep rank. Jehoaida did not contend to be the king, but joyfully took the position of a king-maker.

The Result

Here is the result of the seven-year plan which led to the enthronement of King Jehoash who reigned and did what was right in the sight of God for forty years that Jehoiada the priest instructed him.

2 Kings 12: 1-2
In the seventh year of Jehu, Joash became king, and he reigned in Jerusalem forty years. His mother's name was Zibiah; she was from Beersheba.
Joash did what was right in the eyes of the Lord all the years Jehoiada the priest instructed him.

Testimony: The Entrance Of The Kingdom Citizens Into The Political Circle Of Ile-Oluji Local Government, Ondo, Nigeria By Engineer T. J Akinrelere.

Preamble

The Prophet Isaiah declares in Isaiah 26:2 "**Open ye the gates that the righteous nation which keepteth the truth may enter in**" (KJV)

Democracy as we all know is defined as the government of the people by the people for the people. However, in Nigeria and most parts of Africa, it has been and is still "government of the few people by few people for few people". The situation is made worst as people struggle to join the few who hold onto power by selling their souls to Satan to attain to power at all cost because of quick and corrupt gratification. In essence, this means the political landscape and governance in general is controlled by men and women with demonic power and covenants with Satan and his agents. It was against this background that the Intercessors For Nigeria (IFN), Ondo State Chapter, received a revelation of the above prophetic scripture of Isaiah sometime in 1988/1999.

Under the leadership of Apostle Gbenga Adegbenro, who was the Ondo State Coordinator then, members were instructed to go out into different gates of the State, Offices, Markets, Palaces, Churches, and other Altars etc. to declare this prophetic word of God in order to open the gates for the righteous nations to enter in. A few months after this prayer project in early 1999, elections were held in the nation and a God-fearing man in the person of Late Chief Adebayo Adefarati was elected governor of Ondo State. I could remember that I personally followed Apostle Gbenga Adegbenro to pray with the Governor then in his house at Oba-Ile Housing Estate, in Akure immediately after he was declared the governor-elect.

Family Background and Our Involvement

I am from a very large and well-known family that has as its head a fearless and truthful, God-fearing man. So, one particular trait inherent in our family is TRUTH. I was properly disciple and mentored by the leadership of IFN. Then, I have a burden like that of NEHEMIAH (Neh. 1:1-5), regarding politics and governance in my state. I was commissioned by the IFN leaders to go and participate actively in the politics of my community, Ile-Oluji. As at this time the State and Local Government elections had been held whereas the State/National Assemblies and Presidential elections were yet to be conducted.

Then, only three main political parties namely, Alliance for Democracy (AD), People Democratic Party (PDP) and APP were in existence in our state. The entire South Western States Local Council elections were won by the Alliance for Democracy party with the lone exception of my own Local Government, Ile-Oluji/Okeigbo L.G.A. Otherwise, our state is an AD state. I was led to join the AD political party as it became a burden to well-meaning sons and daughters of the land that AD should win the election in our local government area.

It was at his point that I met with two of my elder brothers (Hon. Dr. Afolabi Akinrelere of blessed memory and Hon. Cornelius A.Akinrelere) to discuss how we can participate in the political affairs of our community and open the gate for righteous people.

There and then we decided that Late Hon. Dr. Afolabi Akinrelere should contest for the State House of Assembly Election. Meanwhile, another senior brother of mine, Hon Bob Akinrelere had been actively involved in politics then and he was the Local Government Chairman of the All Progressive Party (APP) as at that time.

Our First Point of Call – the Throne of the Land

Our first point of call was the Palace, where we were advised out of sincerity and concern, not to involve ourselves in politics for a major reason that politics is dirty and that we may tarnish the sterling reputation of our family by involvement in such a cunning business full of lies and deceit. Moreover, they said that we do not have the money needed to buy votes. The palace counsel was taken in good faith but we were not deterred. I must say here that when we eventually won the election the first congratulatory message was from the same palace. They were amazed to witness such a dramatic turn of event. They could not believe that we could take on the might and stature of the wicked and corrupt political system and win.

Prayer Altar Raised in Our Family House

This is where the church and the house of prayer are very important. The house of prayer and the church were properly mobilized in unity for prayers to take over the government. A prayer altar was raised at our family house which also served as the campaign office. Intensive prayers and prophetic actions were carried out throughout the electioneering period. Interestingly, often our followers on the campaign train would follow me in carrying out prophetic actions.

During the campaign, I would prophesy to the trees, forest, hills, rocks, and rivers, and they too would do the same. It was indeed a case of light versus darkness, as our major political opponents were busy carrying out evil sacrifices at different junctions throughout the Local Government Areas and communities. At different times we were pressured to swear to an oath, requested to engage in sorcery or carry out ungodly sacrifice but we took our stand. Instead, we used the opportunity to witness to the people that there is a better sacrifice that has been made already that is superior to any other sacrifice – the sacrifice of the blood of Jesus.

God so honoured and glorified Himself that later, many confessions were made to different evil actions that were perpetrated against my person that God frustrated and caused to be unfruitful. No doubt a Christian politician must be spiritually equipped and fortified otherwise he or she could fall prey to the devil. We coordinated our campaigns around the prayer altar and normally moved from this prayer altar to go for campaign activities.

Election Day

Basically, each political party is expected to have an agent or two at every polling unit and collation centres, and also at the Independent National Electoral Commission (INEC) office. Unfortunately, most of these agents often compromise and are lured into betraying their candidates for a price. Also, many polling units are prone to rigging, vandalisation, vote buying, and other like vices.

There was an instance where a particular councillorship candidate's wife was offered a free meal that had been mixed with sleeping drugs. She only woke up when the election results were being announced. In our own case, we pre-empted the whole exercise through God's wisdom and forestalled the party to prevent such happenings. How? We brought in our brothers from the House of Prayer to be our agents. Family members volunteered themselves to man polling units. These brethren and family members were well dressed, uncompromising, bold and fearless as against the usual practice of engaging miscreants, thugs, and illiterates who can easily sell out. This was another major strategy that made winning the election a possibility.

There was a dramatic episode in a particular polling unit which changed the course of the election by preventing a rigging attempt. At this polling unit, our beloved brother and member of the house of prayer, Brother Lasbery Njoku was the agent in Ward 5, Bamikemo Community, he had an unforgettable encounter with a notable elderly politician known for sorcery, thuggery and rigging elections. Our brother did not know who this old man was because he did not grow up in our community. For many years, this man determined who wins elections in our local government. That day, he came wearing amulets, carrying live tortoise and all manner of charms, and made several incantations.

Brother Lasbery Njoku was unmoved. He responded by speaking in tongues and declaratory prayers. The old man resulted into physical assault which proved futile. He left with embarrassment, shame and disappointment. He went around other polling units but was prevented from carrying out his evil scheme by our agents in much the same way he was prevented in Ward 5. In fact, our opponents went around spreading rumours that we hired Director of State Security (DSS) personnel as our agents because they noticed all our agents put on nice suits, ties and well-tailored clothing; whereas the normal practice was to wear rough and tattered clothes in preparation and anticipation to rough handle opponents.

Our opponent who had thought the election would be a walkover as we were seen as greenhorns had to leave the town before the announcement of the result. He had already bought live cows and goats, prepared food and drinks, engaged a live band to celebrate his victory. He had confidence in his rigging mechanisms that he had been using successfully for years. This was not to be as our candidate Late Hon. Dr. Afolabi Akinrelere was declared the winner. He was subsequently sworn in as a member of the Ondo State House of Assembly, Ile-Oluji/Okeigbo Consistency. Until death took him from us, Late Honourable Dr. Afolabi Akinrelere was noted for righteousness and justice in the state assembly, government and governance in the Local Government and Ondo State as a whole.

He became a notable peacemaker and created a better environment for others to aspire to political office. This became a turning point and consequently, the AD political party that was in a comatose state in our Local Government was revived and subsequent elections were won by the party. The leader of the Party in our Local Government was impressed and enlisted me as an adviser. In a short while, I became a formidable leader within the party providing leadership and direction. As a result of God's favour, the party chairman gave me the liberty to operate and asked me to go and mobilize other men and women of integrity and who feared God to join the party. As a result men and women of proven integrity were integrated into the political structure of the state to the glory of God and the benefits of mankind.

Talking About Strategic Planning and Actionable Process

Looking at the strategic plan and processes that was put in place to take back the throne from Athaliah, we see diligence in the strategy of Jehoiada which produced good results. This was a good response and solution to a problem in the Nation. In the end, everyone rejoiced when Athaliah was taken out of the throne after six years of wickedness and devastation. This intervention by Jehoiada the priest was one of our motivations to move into action and risk our lives because we believed we must take action and calculated risks to achieve our desired goal. This attitude and strategy is what we need to replicate in every community in Africa and globally to overthrow wicked and oppressive leaders.

We need to discern the men and women that God has chosen and put the right strategies in place. If there's no adequate and proper preparation there's no way a righteous leader can take the throne and lead righteously. Jehoiada took time to strategize. It took him six years of planning; it took us two years of planning and implementation. He only started implementing his plan in the seventh year. When Athaliah took the throne and established wickedness on the throne she could not be challenged immediately. Instead of doing nothing, Jehoiada strategized and mobilized the people and the priesthood. Together with fervent prayers, we need to put strategies and formidable structures in place to overthrow the wicked and put righteous people in authority.

For any move of God such as the enthronement of righteous governance especially on the African continent, and elsewhere we must make sure that they are is a built-up and strong structure on the ground so that we can be able to establish good governance. Prayer alone cannot do everything. We need proper structure, strategy and action. Together with dynamic, prevailing and continuous prayer, equal emphasis should be on building viable and solid organizational and political structure on the ground putting things on the ground to run when the time is right to run

Conquering Fear

Jehoiada put his life at stake. He conquered fear. He didn't allow the fear to incapacitate him. Behind the scene, he was instructing the priests and he was prepared to face Athaliah when the time was right. When it comes to the issue of thrones, government and good governance, we need to conquer fear to be able to go all the way and carry out bold initiatives courageously. For us to be able to replicate what Jehoiada did in his time, we had to follow this brave example in order to challenge the status quo in our territories. Brother Lasbery Njoku showed this kind of bravery in the testimony iterated above, demonstrating that this orientation works today. With this kind of training, boldness, courage and orientation, we can systematically take over community by community, kingdom by kingdom and nation by nation.

Family Structure

Joash, the rightful heir and king that Athaliah usurped was hidden as a child and brought up in the way of the Lord in the family. The importance of training children as royal personalities within the families is very crucial. Family is a very important framework and structure of God's government on earth. Our parents taught us the fear of God, righteousness and justice. Most people in our community know our family for forthrightness which made it easy for us to be easily accepted by good people in the community. The work must begin from the family government to train the children to do righteousness and justice because it will have an impact on what God wants to achieve in the land and the nations.

Building A Network

Your network is your net worth. It is very crucial to assess the purpose and utility of each and every person in this kind of assignment and to build a good network of people with like minds. Everyone was given a purpose and a function to fulfil during this move. We need to know where each and everyone must operate and which gates they need to possess. We need to be careful to involve people who are trustworthy and people who are loyal to God and His agenda for thrones. This was still part of the strategy. Joash was hidden by people who understood the move of God. He was not king yet, but he was being prepared. In many instances, we cry out to God, but we do not have leaders who are properly prepared, groomed and mentored that will be able to take the throne with the capacity and courage to effect transformation and good governance.

Let Us Arise and Build

I like to conclude this chapter with the call that was made to everyone in the days of Nehemiah, the builder who rebuilt the walls of Jerusalem. Nehemiah realized that the task of building the wall and establishing good governance could not be done all by himself. He made a clarion call and persuaded other leaders to work together with him. He persuaded them by articulating the vision of a righteous and secure nation, just as I have done in this book until all shared it and committed themselves to it.

'Let us rise up and build'.

22.

THRONES, NATIONAL TRANSFORMATION AND GOOD GOVERNANCE

Over the years, the term "good governance" has gained currency as an ideal of human attainment and the subject matter of critical global discourse. At the same time, it has become a staple of development literature and profound debate in academic and political discourse. A throne or government is established by God to bring order and progress in society for the flourishing of human beings and the environment. Hence, thrones are vital to the transformation and sustainability of kingdoms, communities and nations. Kings and leaders rule or govern territories with authority from the thrones. Therefore, territories and nations need men and women of impeccable character to occupy the thrones – This is a major challenge in establishing good governance among the nations.

Ideally, God expects earthly thrones, the seat of government of nations to be an extension of His Throne and for earthly kings and leaders in every domain to draw wisdom, counsels, blueprints and strategies from Him to transform their kingdoms, communities and nations. However, this is not so in most cases because Biblical principles are not usually factored into matters of political governance. The idea and belief system that morality has no place in political governance is from the pit of hell. Rather, a territory or a nation can only be established, sustained and developed through the moral conduct and integrity of its king or leader.

"By justice a king gives a country stability, but those who are greedy for bribes tear it down". Proverbs 29:4

Moreover, there are thrones of iniquity and wickedness that have been established in territories and nations through human interface with satanic forces and ideologies that must be overthrown before we can establish a righteous government. We need to deal with the corrupt culture and wicked thrones that manipulate kings and leaders to do wickedness.

Governance

The concept of governance is not new, as stated above; government and governance have been put in place by the Creator Himself. However, in academic debate and political discourse, there is no universally accepted definition of Governance when used in political literature. The word governance comes from the Greek word "kubernaein" and the Latin verb "gubernare" which means "to steer", "to guide", "lead", and "pilot" in the context of steering and leading men. Having the same linguistic root, the term was often used interchangeably with the term "government". The World Bank views governance as "the manner in which power is exercised in the management of a country's economic and social resources for development (World Bank, Governance, Washington, D.C, 1993). The focus of World Bank here is primarily political governance in terms of management, economy and distribution of resources for the development of the state.

However, The United Nations Development Programme (UNDP), defines governance as "the exercise of economic, political and administrative authority to manage a country's affairs at all levels. It comprises the mechanisms, processes and institutions through which citizens and groups articulate their interests, exercise their legal rights, meet their obligations and mediate their differences" (UNDP, Governance for Sustainable Human Development, UNDP Policy Document, New York, 1977). For the EU, governance concerns "the state's ability to serve the citizens. It refers to the rules, processes and behaviour by which interests are articulated, resources are managed, and power is exercised in society."

In general, we can look at governance as the process of making and implementing decisions within an organization or a nation. Governance encompasses how a government rules her state, the political process, the setting of rules and enforcement of laws and order to steer the functioning and development of an organization or society. Basically, governance has to do with an organization or a government and how it runs her state.

Good Governance

Nowadays, 'good governance' is being increasingly used in development discourse. Bad governance is being increasingly regarded as one of the root causes of all evil among the nations. Again, as with governance, there is no internationally agreed definition of good governance. However, it relates to the political and institutional processes and outcomes that are necessary to achieve the goals of development.

The United Nations has described good governance with EIGHT major characteristics: In that construct, good governance must be **participatory, consensus-oriented, accountable, transparent, responsive, effective and efficient, equitable and inclusive and follows the rule of law.**

According to the Council of Europe (2008), good governance is the responsible conduct of public affairs and management of public resources as encapsulated in 12 principles of good governance:

1. Participation, Representation, Fair Conduct of Elections.
2. Responsiveness.
3. Efficiency and Effectiveness.
4. Openness and Transparency.
5. Rule of Law.
6. Ethical Conduct.
7. Competence and Capacity.
8. Innovation and Openness to Change.
9. Sustainability and Long-Term Orientation.
10. Sound Financial Management.
11. Human Rights, Cultural Diversity and Social Cohesion.
12. Accountability.

In general, good governance is considered key to achieving sustainable development and human well-being. The core views expressed in defining good governance is that corruption and wrongdoing are minimized, but they concluded that this is an ideal which is difficult to achieve in its totality.

The issue is that a nation may have a good constitution, sound policies and principles as encapsulated by the Council of Europe; nonetheless the operators of these policies and the complex dynamics of thrones are the critical factors responsible for either bad governance or good governance. You cannot determine what a human being will do until you give them power and money.

In the preface to his famous book, From Third World to First World: The Singapore Story; Lee Kwan Yew wrote concerning Public order: *"We cannot afford to forget that public order, personal security, economic and social progress, and prosperity are not the natural order of things that they depend on ceaseless effort and attention from an honest and effective government that the people must elect."* As documented in the book, Lee demonstrated the extraordinary efforts, the arduous process and the determination required to transform a nation and establish good governance.

God and Good Governance

- God's principles, commandments, laws, testimony, statutes, judgement and the fear of the LORD are all about Good Governance as stated wonderfully in Psalms 19.
- The Bible (The Owner's Manual) is all about kings, leaders and leadership principles, government and good Governance. Good governance is upholding the moral standards and principles as laid out by God.
- Doing what is right and establishing justice are the foundations of good governance which are the foundations of God's Throne
- The problem is that the basic principles and foundations of good governance clearly established in the word of God are ignored and replaced with human philosophy and demonic ideologies with the hope that we can better manage our affairs without God.
- Psalm 72 presents God's perspective in the form of prayer to guide kings, rulers and leaders so that there will be peace and prosperity in the land.

"Give the king Your judgments, O God, and Your righteousness to the king's Son. He will judge Your people with righteousness, and Your poor with justice....For He will deliver the needy when he cries, the poor also, and him who has no helper. He will spare the poor and needy, and will save the souls of the needy. He will redeem

their life from oppression and violence; and precious shall be their blood in His sight". Psalm 72:1-2, 12-14

- It offers an ideal governance model, focused on a relationship of care for the poor and vulnerable.
- Good governance is based on the principles of justice, righteousness and compassion, defending the rights of the poor and marginalised and protecting the people from destruction, provision of safe and enabling environment for the people and establishing the land sustainably.
- In sum, according to the Bible, good political governance involves upholding moral standards as laid out by God who created government on the earth. Any deviation from these standards is misrule and misgovernance.

Self-Governance and Good Governance

- Self-governance is the exercise of power or control over oneself without external interference
- Self-mastery is self-government or self-control, the foundation of a strong character, growth, and good values. If a person cannot govern himself, cannot control his/her passions, he/she is dangerous to the society.
- "Whoever has no rule over his own spirit is like a city broken down, without walls." Proverbs 25:28
- "He who is slow to anger is better than the mighty, and he who rules his spirit than he who takes a city." Proverbs 16:32
- A comparison of the two proverbs reveals the great importance of self-control or self-governance as both an offensive and defensive attribute that enhances good leadership and good governance.
- With self-governance is personal security and identity. An identity crisis brings insecurity to a person and invariably it can ruin his or her domain of influence.
- You are either a part of the problem or you become part of the solution. To achieve good governance, start by governing your affairs properly

Family Governance and Good Governance

- The family is government and an extension of God's Throne on the earth. Good governance must begin at the family level and homesteads, starting the battle for good governance from the grassroots. The family is the most important good governance delivery system."*For I know him, that he will command his children and his household after him, and they shall keep the way of the LORD, to do justice and judgment; that the LORD may bring upon Abraham that which he hath spoken of him*". Genesis 18:19.

- Any nation that loses the battle of good governance at the family level will end up wasting her resources to keep criminals in jail and rehabilitating drug addicts. They will continue to waste huge resources on security and violence will not cease from the nation. This is a brutal truth that we need to address in order to rescue our nations from bad governance. When nations are governed by men and women of questionable upbringing and character, you can only imagine when such people are given position, power and influence.

- And he said unto them, "*Set your hearts unto all the words which I testify among you this day, which ye shall command your children to observe to do, all the words of this law. For it is not a vain thing for you; because it is your life: and through this thing ye shall prolong your days in the land, whither ye go over Jordan to possess it*". Deut. 32:46,47

- Attitude and mind-set are the most difficult thing to change in life because it is the totality of the processes of an individual's upbringing. Once the foundation of family values is compromised and corrupted, it will end up in corruption in the society. You can imagine a child brought up in a family and taught to hate people of other tribes; what do you think will happen when they get to a position of power? Healing of nations and good governance development must start from the healing of families.

Sonship, Nobility and Good Governance

As long as the heir to the throne or position of authority is a child, he is not different from a slave and you cannot rule or govern with slave mentality. Childishness and slave mentality is a mental attitude that includes feelings of inferiority; characterized by poor values systems and bad decisions. According to Ecclesiastes 10:16, 17; the character of a King or a leader matters whether a king or a leader is of noble character or not.

"Woe to you, O Land, when your king is a child, and your princes feast in the morning
Blessed are you, O Land, when your king is the son of nobles, and your princes feast at the proper time – for strength and not for drunkenness!"

This is a teaching to remind us of the significance of wise and capable leaders and the influence of their behaviour on their territories and society. Virtually everything that truly qualifies a person for good leadership and good governance is directly linked to good character. The prosperity of a land, a community and a nation depends on the character of its leaders. The idea of a child is not a matter of age but of childishness characterised by foolishness, weakness, gluttony, self-indulgence, slothfulness and bad decisions. Childish character will bring disaster to a nation and any domain of influence. It is bad for a land, community and nation to be led by foolish and self-indulgent kings and leaders. Consider the example of Rehoboam who was a young and inexperienced king: Instead of listening to the voice of experience, Rehoboam chose to listen to his young, selfish friends; and it brought a major disaster to the nation. 1 King 12:1-11 The elders of Israel had made Rehoboam king after the death of his father Solomon. No doubt, Solomon was a great king with regards to good administration, but Solomon engaged the people with heavy taxation and forced services. The people demanded relief from the heavy yoke for their total allegiance to him. Then, the king consulted the elders who stood before his father Solomon and they counselled him: "If you will be a servant to these people today, and serve them, and answer them, and speak good words to them, then they will be your servants forever." 1 Kings 12:7. But Rehoboam rejected the advice of the wise elders and consulted the young men who had grown up with him. The younger men offered advice contrary to the wise counsels of the elders. Rehoboam answered the elders of Israel roughly and did not listen to the people. The elders rejected Rehoboam, the kingdom was divided and the elders took Jeroboam as king over the ten northern kingdoms. Rehoboam's actions and childishness brought a great devastation to the nation.

Kingly Character Development

In the words of King Lemuel's mother written in Proverbs 31:1-9, there are rules about actions and activities that people in authority should or should not perform or take part in. Here, a king recounts what he learned from his mother. The king's mother taught her son what it takes to be a person of good character and a noble king.

- What, my son? And what, the son of my womb? And what, the son of my vows?
- Do not give your strength to women, nor your ways to that which destroys kings.
- Do not use your authority as a means of debauchery.
- Keep your head clear from the stupefying effects of alcohol.
- Use your power and authority to help the poor and powerless.
- This is the vow and passion for training and raising sons and nobles for good governance.

When The Righteous Are in Authority the People Rejoice – Prov. 29:2

It is to the benefit of the community or nation when the righteous are in authority which means when the righteous govern, the entire people and land will rejoice, but the rule of the wicked brings lawlessness, increases violence and the entire community or nation suffers. From the above, from what has been written in this and from our practical engagements with kings and leaders in various leadership positions, we posit that we need to look at three concepts for sustainable development and good governance among the nations:

1. **Personality** – Personal good character development and how to raise a righteous personality for a position of authority is a critical challenge to good governance.

Big Question: Can we find such a one as this? Genesis 41:38. The number one challenge about good governance has been: can we find such a one as this; a man in whom the Spirit of God is? Today, nations are plagued with a legion of men and women not fit to counsel kindergarten, yet our kings and leaders are often subjected to their influence. But Joseph, by the Spirit and the wisdom of God was able to lay down and implement fourteen years' development agenda for Egypt as Prime Minister of Egypt.

Another big question: are you a man or a woman of integrity? All matters of national transformation and good governance are subject to this basic ingredient: integrity of heart. Before you point accusing fingers to others, are you a man or a woman of integrity in your private and public life? Private and public life disparity is a serious challenge in this digital age. The battle for good governance must begin with you in your private and public life being in harmony with integrity. National transformation and nation's building is by integrity of heart and it must be built from within

Examine Yourself and Prepare for Good Governance

- Let every man and every woman examine himself or herself before taking on a position of authority and be truthful to yourself. Are you truthful?
- Can people count on you as a person of integrity?
- Are you honest with yourself and others?
- Can you be trusted? Are you dependable and trustworthy?
- Are you armed to justify yourself or are you willing to trust God and his word to help you overcome the deceitfulness of your own heart?
- No hiding place, the challenges and the temptations of the thrones will reveal who you are.

The Fear of the LORD and Good Governance

In the last words of King David, he wrote an admonition that anyone that rules over men must be just ruling in the fear of God – 2 Samuel 23:3. Nehemiah, the builder demonstrated the critical issue in personal character development and good governance which he described as the fear of the LORD. "For the entire twelve years that I was governor of

Judah—from the twentieth year to the thirty-second year of the reign of King Artaxerxes—neither I nor my officials drew on our official food allowance. The former governors, in contrast, had laid heavy burdens on the people, demanding a daily ration of food and wine, besides forty pieces of silver. Even their assistants took advantage of the people. **But because I feared God**, I did not act that way. I also devoted myself to working on the wall and refused to acquire any land. And I required all my servants to spend time working on the wall." Nehemiah 5: 14-16. Nehemiah refused to abuse his authority because he feared God, and the fear of God is the beginning of wisdom. This is a reminder for leaders to act responsibly when in positions of power. The fear of God offers valuable wisdom and insights for individuals in leadership roles, whether in the family, community, religious, corporate organizations, or the nation. The question then is: is your heart established in the fear of God?

2. The Throne's Entity, Identity and Foundations
Taking a look at what happened to the nation of Israel when King David was on the throne, a man after God's own heart despite good administration, yet the nation suffered famine for three and a half years. That is to say, added to raising leaders with impeccable characters on the throne we need to know that the throne is an entity with its own identity and foundations which of course can either enhance or diminish good governance. Obviously, King David inherited a throne with foundations of bloodshed which at first he did not redeem his throne from blood guiltiness.

- There are fundamentals and dynamics of thrones that we need to understand and deploy with wisdom and practical applications to facilitate good governance
- This is a typical example while a good leader with good intentions may still be hindered in their throne assignments if the faulty foundations are not properly addressed.
- This also may be responsible for the reason why some kings and leaders will start well, but they may fail at the end.
- This has been well articulated in chapters eight and eighteen of this book.

3. Political Process Engagement

Another challenge to good governance is the lack of engagement in the political processes by the Christian community to get the righteous into positions of authority. The understanding of the concept of thrones and government by the generality of the people especially the Christian communities has not helped matters at all. Again, in some African countries, to get righteous men and women to the position of authority in order to establish good governance is like fighting for a new independence. Moreover, the political processes involve huge amounts of resources that most people with good intentions find difficult to afford. Nevertheless, there is a need for a new orientation and paradigm and we need help to be able to oust corrupt culture and systems.

Conclusion

- Righteous government, good governance, economic and sustainable development do not come by easily; we need to be intentional, proactive, dedicated and be prepared to pay the price.
- We need blueprints and strategies to raise righteous kings/leaders
- We need to get to the roots of bad leadership especially in Africa
- We need to deal with faulty foundations of thrones – Redeeming the thrones
- We need to teach integrity of heart and skilfulness of hands as instruments for national transformation
- We need to commence training and teaching on the fear of the LORD
- We need to seriously begin the battle for good governance from the family
- This is not rhetoric, but a call to be intentional and deliberate in strategic planning and implementation of strategies over a period of time.

23.

DETERMINATION AND RESOLUTION FOR GOOD GOVERNANCE

Psalm 101: Commitment To Live and Rule Righteously

This Psalm serves as a remarkable commitment to living a life of personal integrity, righteous rule and good governance in alignment with divine principles. It challenges us to pursue integrity in our private and family lives, to shun wickedness, and to commit to morality in public life, walking with integrity to establish good governance. In this Psalm, King David declares the intimate resolve of a leader to lead with integrity and a steadfast heart. It is a proclamation, expressing a ruler's commitment to godly principles and the denouncement of wickedness in all its forms.

The themes – God's sovereignty, personal commitment to God, personal integrity and wholesome character, mercy and justice, ethical living, denouncement of the wicked and their wickedness, rewarding the righteous, morality in public life and righteous leadership are all the fundamental themes of good governance. King David had a burning and abiding desire for integrity to define his reign and the entire nation. Therefore, he fiercely made a solemn vow and commitment to God to rule with integrity in his private life, family life (household) and the kingdom (society). King David was proactive in his resolutions and his desire to see integrity in the entire nation. This is an excellent model for a Godly government and good governance that is applicable to everyone and families. It instructs all that are in any position of power and authority; small or great, to be resolute in their commitment to personal integrity and use their power and influence to establish good governance in their domain of influence. Integrity brings blessings to a nation, while the lack of integrity brings a nation down.

Nehemiah's Godly Example

As a governor of Judah for twelve years, Nehemiah did not demand the governor's provisions when he could have, instead, he also gave generously from his own personal resources.

"Moreover from the time that I was appointed to be their governor in the land of Judah, from the twentieth year even unto the two and thirtieth year of Artaxerxes the king, that is, twelve years, I and my brethren have not eaten the bread of the governor. But the former governors that had been before me were chargeable unto the people, and had taken of them bread and wine, beside forty shekels of silver; yea, even their servants bare rule over the people: but so did not I, because of the fear of God. Yea, also I continued in the work of this wall, neither bought we any land: and all my servants were gathered thither unto the work. Moreover there were at my table an hundred and fifty of the Jews and rulers, beside those that came unto us from among the heathen that are about us. Now that which was prepared for me daily was one ox and six choice sheep; also fowls were prepared for me, and once in ten days store of all sorts of wine: yet for all this required not I the bread of the governor, because the bondage was heavy upon this people". Nehemiah 5:14-18.

As attested to here, Nehemiah did what every godly ruler must do.

Late President Hage G. Geingob of Namibia

Late President Geingob was elected as the president of Namibia in March 2015, he started well in line with the principles of good governance by his resolve to lead by example a clean administration and an anti-corruption government. He started by declaring his personal assets and encouraged all his cabinet ministers to do the same. In addition, he personally carried out fitness assessments for his ministers for their suitability as office bearers. Moreover, the president demonstrated his passion for the poor and the needy in that he publicly committed to giving twenty percent of his income to help the poor and the needy. President Geingob's example at the onset of his government demonstrates that Nehemiah's example is practicable in our contemporary times.

King David's Resolve And Determination (Psalm 101:1-8)

When you critically examine Psalm 101, you will see David as a national king, the specifics concerning his resolve to rule as a Godly king, the specific goals concerning his character and conduct, as well as the officials that will rule with him. King David resolved to operate a clean and righteous reign from top down. This can be achieved in our nations, but it will take strong determination and the help of God.

Psalm 101:1- I will sing of mercy and justice to You, O Lord

King David resolved from the onset that his reign and kingdom will be characterized by mercy and justice. He made a commitment to show kindness and meting out appropriate punishment to those who deserved it. King David was social justice activist. When David got to the throne, he remembered Jonathan, his covenant friend who had died in battle with King Saul, his father.

"And David said, Is there yet any that is left of the house of Saul, that I may shew him kindness for Jonathan's sake? And there was of the house of Saul a servant whose name was Ziba. And when they had called him unto David, the king said unto him, Art thou Ziba? And he said, Thy servant is he. And the king said, Is there not yet any of the house of Saul, that I may shew the kindness of God unto him? And Ziba said unto the king, Jonathan hath yet a son, which is lame on his feet. And the king said unto him, Where is he? And Ziba said unto the king, Behold, he is in the house of Machir, the son of Ammiel, in Lo-debar. Then king David sent, and fetched him out of the house of Machir, the son of Ammiel, from Lo-debar. Now when Mephibosheth, the son of Jonathan, the son of Saul, was come unto David, he fell on his face, and did reverence. And David said, Mephibosheth. And he answered, Behold thy servant! And David said unto him, Fear not: for I will surely shew thee kindness for Jonathan thy father's sake, and will restore thee all the land of Saul thy father; and thou shalt eat bread at my table continually. And he bowed himself, and said, What is thy servant, that thou shouldest look upon such a dead dog as I am? Then the king called to Ziba, Saul's servant, and said unto him, I have given unto thy master's son all that pertained to Saul and to all his house. Thou

therefore, and thy sons, and thy servants, shall till the land for him, and thou shalt bring in the fruits, that thy master's son may have food to eat: but Mephibosheth thy master's son shall eat bread always at my table...2 Samuel 9:1-13

Psalm 101:2 – I Will Behave Wisely in a Perfect Way

"I will behave wisely in a perfect way.... I will walk within my house with a perfect heart" King David vowed and committed himself to impeccable character of personal integrity and self-control. He prioritized a deep desire to live a blameless life characterized by uprightness, wholeness or integrity. The emphasis here is on the heart, a resolve that his intentions, motives and objectives will be pure and without hypocrisy, or deceit.

He made up his mind to be genuine and authentic both in his private and public life. No separation between his personal life and his official life; the private, as well as the public. David understood that what a man is in private will affect how he leads in public. This principle is critical for rulers and everyone in position of authority to understand. This principle is solidly established in the Bible as the requirements for elders and deacons in 1 Timothy 3:1-5. "This is a faithful saying: If a man desires the position of a bishop, he desires a good work. A bishop then must be blameless, the husband of one wife, temperate, sober-minded, of good behaviour, hospitable, able to teach; not given to wine, not violent, not greedy for money, but gentle, not quarrelsome, not covetous; one who rules his own house well, having his children in submission with all reverence (for if a man does not know how to rule his own house, how will he take care of the church of God?);..."

Psalm 101:3 – I Will Set Nothing Wicked Before My Eyes

"I will set nothing wicked before my eyes; I hate the work of those who fall away; It shall not cling to me." Power dynamics exposes leaders to various vices and lusts. The eyes are the gateway to the soul and diverse lust. If you want to have a consistent righteous government, be careful what you set your eyes to look at or watch. Discipline over the eyes is a significant measure to succeed on the throne and every aspect of human endeavour. Job demonstrated his pious lifestyle by a commitment with a covenant not to look upon a young woman in impure ways in Job 31:1. "I have made a covenant with my eyes; why then should I look upon a young woman? It takes great resolve and discipline as a person in position of power to ignore and set aside to lure and allure of sin and wickedness.

Psalm 101:4 – A Perverse Heart Shall Depart from Me

"A perverse heart shall depart from me; I will not know wickedness." It takes great determination to pursue and stand for righteousness. Your personal resolve to not practice wickedness must be accompanied with a resolve to not keep wicked people as officials. There must be a determination not to tolerate evil people around you. If you want to be consistent in your personal life, you must stay away from the appearance of evil and evil company.

Psalm 101:5 – Whoever secretly slanders his neighbour, him I will destroy.

"Whoever secretly slanders his neighbour, Him I will destroy; the one who has a haughty look and a proud heart, Him I will not endure." This is a critical instruction to determine not to tolerate slanderers, those who damage others people's reputation by making false statement about them to gain favour. Their trademark is to cause discord. The Bible teaches that it is unwise to even associate with slanderers (Proverbs 20:19). Again, one root why people slanders others is pride; whereas humility is the hallmark of a great leader. You must be diligent enough as a leader to get rid of slanderers and the proud in heart because commitment to public morality demands that leaders practice humility, and carefully cultivate and vet the company they keep.

Psalm 101:6 – My eyes shall be on the faithful of the land.

"My eyes shall be on the faithful of the land, That they may dwell with me; He who walks in a perfect way, He shall serve me." You are as good as the people you surround yourself with in any leadership position. If your desire and focus is to establish justice and good governance, you must look for and surround yourself with the faithful in the land. Look for the faithful of the land and set them up as leaders. People who will not defeat the end of justice, but value and defend justice in the land.

The Jethro Principle: "But select capable men from all the people–men who fear God, trustworthy men who hate dishonest gain–and appoint them as officials over thousands, hundreds, fifties and tens". Exodus 18:21 (NIV). When you are a king or a leader in a position of authority, you need other leaders who can get the job done. This is the model for effective leadership and government. The principle here underscores the importance of character, truthfulness and justice in leaders.

Psalm 101:7 – He who works deceit shall not dwell within my house.
"He who works deceit shall not dwell within my house; He who tells lies shall not continue in my presence". The challenge with leadership positions sometimes is how to get and maintain others who are uncompromising and loyal. For your leadership and your domain to be characterised by justice at all levels, you must be ruthless with those who practice deceit and tell lies. Corrupt officials must be summarily dealt with.

Psalm 101:8 – Early I will destroy all the wicked of the land.
"Early I will destroy all the wicked of the land, that I may cut off all the evildoers from the city of the Lord". In the determination to rule righteously and establish good governance, the wicked must be promptly removed without delay. A leader must not delay in making this decision. Some of these decisions may seem difficult to make and implement, that is why you begin with personal integrity to be able to take bold decisions to summarily deal with the wicked of the land.

Prayers to Walk with Integrity

1. God, I pray for integrity.
2. Let my life both in private and public be marked by walking with integrity of heart.
3. Deliver me, I pray from deceit, hypocrisy and inauthenticity.
4. Deliver my eyes from worthless things and lust
5. Help me to walk with integrity of heart before you in my house, when I am alone.
6. Help me to walk with integrity in my public engagements and life.

Conclusion

Accountability in the acts of good governance is a solemn pledge that everyone must engage with; both in private and public life in order to establish righteous governance in all spheres of society. I adjure you to start right now to strive to live a life of personal integrity, public morality and accountability. To teach your family and household righteousness and justice, to stand for justice everywhere there is injustice. By doing so, you are contributing to good governance. Good governance is everybody's responsibility and it is never too late to begin where you are right now.

24.

OPERATING ON THE THRONES GLOBAL MOVEMENT

Global Initiative for Transformation of Nations

In the year 2020, God laid on my heart a burden to start an initiative and training on operating on thrones in order to facilitate the process of establishing righteous government and good governance. It was launched online with traditional rulers and kings (monarchs), government and political leaders as well as leaders from various domains of influence. This is an initiative to intentionally and strategically raise men and women for the thrones who are fully equipped with the wisdom, integrity of heart and skilfulness of hands, and all that is required to operate effectively on the thrones or any position of authority in order to establish righteousness and justice and to positively transform their domains, kingdoms and spheres of influence. God's plan is always about raising righteous rulers and leaders:

"Behold, the days are coming," says the LORD, "That I will raise to David a Branch of righteousness; A King shall reign and prosper, And execute judgment and righteousness in the earth. In His days Judah will be saved, And Israel will dwell safely; Now this is His name by which He will be called: THE LORD OUR RIGHTEOUSNESS.

The focus in the above scripture is on our Lord and Saviour Jesus Christ. However, God's focus throughout all ages is on raising good and righteous kings and leaders who will reign in righteousness and prosper by executing justice in the land. To raise good leaders and establish righteous thrones involves seeking strategies and blueprints from the heart of God, discipleship training and mentoring of men and women, young and old, developing productive plans and processes, and implementation of short-term and long-term strategies for the enthronement of a righteous generations of men and women in order to establish Godly and good governance among the nations.

This global initiative is a project that will deploy a multidimensional and multifaceted approach to socio-spiritual and socio-economic interventions in our communities towards the rebuilding of the waste places, the desolations of many generations and the establishment of enduring processes that over time will bring righteousness, justice and transformation to our communities, land and nations. This will require raising men and women with the sceptre of righteousness in families, communities, cities, businesses, workplaces, marketplaces, government, schools and churches. Good leaders who understand the complex dynamics of thrones and who are committed to reigning in righteousness will bring blessing and development to any nation.

Redefining The Concept of Thrones

For this global movement, we posit that the throne is the position of kings, rulers, government, leaders (religious, corporate and political), parents, guardians and educators whereby someone has the privilege and responsibility to nurture, steer, guide, supervise, direct, lead, oversee and assert authority over others, be it a household, groups of people, community, land, territories and the nation.

Having Good Intentions Alone May Not Create Good Outcomes

We understand that operating righteously on thrones is not the natural order of things in most communities and nations. It requires strong commitment and determination. It does not happen automatically. Merely having good intentions will not create good outcomes. This is why a lot of people who have inherited or taken over positions of leadership, positions of authority and influence or governments of nations have created more problems than solutions. Many will start very well but later turn around to fail woefully.

Others have the mind of doing good when they get to the thrones only to discover they are being hindered from doing the good in their hearts or effect the change that they intended to establish as they, unfortunately, realize that they were not prepared for the spiritual dimensions of thrones as they experience certain invincible forces or powers that are beyond the ordinary once they get to the thrones. All these we have experienced as a ministry in our dealings with kings (monarchs), traditional leaders, and political leaders of many kingdoms. We know that the moral failures and character flaws of many kings and leaders have brought dire consequences on many communities, kingdoms and nations especially the nations of Africa, but now we want to seek the help of God to reverse these trends of colossal waste of leadership potentials and restore the nations to the paths of good government and governance.

The Challenges To Overcome
As part of our strategies, we have identified and outlined the following challenges among others that we need to confront and overcome by the wisdom of God.

- Lack of understanding of the purpose of thrones, nor the throne culture and mindset; the mysteries, dynamics and the operating principles of the thrones that lead to manipulation of kings, thrones and people in authority to do wickedness.
- Lack of spiritual, emotional and intellectual capacity building to facilitate good and righteous governance with the basic ingredients for establishing righteousness, justice and sustainable development on the thrones.
- Deficiencies in strategies to deal with the foundations of thrones and engage with the cleansing of the thrones of kingdoms (ancient and modern) whose foundations produce wicked leaders, bad leadership and promote Babylonian and Satanic agenda among the nations
- Inappropriate and inadequate discipleship training, mentoring and spiritual capacity-building strategies for kings and people in leadership positions to overcome the challenges and responsibilities that go with thrones and when they get there they become casualties of circumstances and powers beyond their control.
- Lack of understanding by kings and leaders as custodians and gatekeepers of kingdom resources to deal with Babylonian systems and bring prosperity to their lands and spheres of influence.

The Thrones Paradigm Shift

The thrones paradigm is a mindset and a concept that each of us is currently responsible for one throne or another. It is a paradigm of initiating transformation by deploying the dynamic power of thrones and the spiritual energies of kings and all people in positions of authority through proper mentorship. It is the paradigm shift of securing the future by raising royal personalities today for future deliverance and transformation of our nation just as Mordecai, the Jew was a dynamic mentor to Esther in the Bible; two people who shaped the history of their nation for good. We must see thrones in the lives of everyone we are opportune to influence wherever we find ourselves today.

Strategic Training and Mentorship

The throne is a place of strategy, power, authority and influence; and the main purpose of the throne is to establish righteousness and justice. However, for people to be effective and successful in their mandate and assignment on the thrones, they must be properly trained, their hearts must be well prepared to establish the purpose of the thrones without compromise. The thrones paradigm must be taught and embraced as a veritable tool and resource for the transformation of communities and nations.

The thrones training, coaching and mentoring must be conceptualized and intentionally programmed into the fabrics of life from birth, in our families, all institutions and government. Fresh vision must be cast to explain the paradigm shift in the operating principles of thrones with emphasis on integrity of heart, skilfulness of hands and the fear of the LORD as the basic ingredients for national transformation and sustainable development. We must engage with the throne paradigm with due diligence and uncommon audacity, blueprints, actionable plans and implementation of both short-term and long-term strategies to unseat the thrones of wickedness in the land and open the gates for the righteous thrones and nations that keep the truth to enter and establish good governance.

Key Features of Operating on The Thrones

- The restoration of the king-priest identity, mandate and capacity of each individual and mentoring people for their throne assignment.
- Redeeming the thrones and dealing with the foundations of thrones that hinders people on the thrones from doing the right things, but rather promotes bad leadership. Establishing the thrones of righteousness everywhere.
- Dealing with the spirits which destroy leaders (kings and royal seeds), removal of wickedness from the thrones of the land, raising, establishing and mentoring the righteous on the thrones in every place.
- Leading with integrity of heart, skilfulness of hands, competence, excellent spirit, dealing with the culture of greed, laziness and corruption, establishing righteousness, administering justice and ruling in the fear of God.
- Establish the fear and the worship of God on the throne, institutionalize pragmatic socio-spiritual and socio-economic interventions and provide solutions to the problems of society.

The Global Thrones Movement

The vision is to raise, equip and release men and women with the sceptre of righteousness to reign on the thrones and transform their domains, communities and nations. When people of similar ideas, interests and burdens come together and share a common vision; the collective synergy automatically brings exponential growth. And with clarity and focus on the shared vision, success means the same for everyone involved and the glory belongs to God. We are prepared to share this global vision and initiatives with as many groups of people whose hearts the Lord has stirred up and are willing to partner with this initiative from kingdom to kingdom, province to province and nation to nation, small or large groups of people in any place and in every nation that can be mobilized which may be in a physical location as well as online. This will involve networking and collaboration with other individuals, groups and existing structures in different places, communities and nations, brainstorming and building strategic relationships on shared vision.

How Can You Be Involved?

You can participate effectively in this global movement in the following ways:

- Mobilize groups of people in your locality, territory or domain of influence for vision sharing and brainstorming
- Make yourself, your family, organization and community available for training in our discipleship training, coaching and mentoring programs
- Share the global initiative with others who can mobilize groups of people for vision sharing and training purposes
- Pray regularly for effective doors to be opened for this initiative among every tribe, and tongue, people and nations
- Let us join hands together to establish righteous government among the nations

THE TIME IS NOW!

The Time is Now!

The time for concerned citizens of various nations to step forward and set up processes and strategies to raise up righteous leaders who will take control of government at all levels with the capacity to establish righteousness and justice.

The Time is Now!

To redefine and change the narrative of bad leadership and misgovernance to righteous leadership and good governance among the nations.

The Time is Now!

To kick start the processes and strategies that will produce the reign of righteousness in all domains of influence in our nations.

The Clarion Call

Are you willing to make an indelible impact in transforming and shaping the history of your domain, kingdom, community or nation? Destiny is corporate and the battle for the thrones is fierce. Be of good courage, let us hold hands strongly together for the cities of our God and let us rise up and build, for we are certain that the hand of God is upon us for good in this matter of thrones. Enough of rhetoric about problems, we need solutions and blueprints that will bring an end to corruption, bad leadership and misgovernance among the nations. There is enough wisdom and strategies to deploy from the Bible, the book of government to establish righteous and good governance in every domain of influence.

REFERENCES

Abati, R (14 October, 2016) 'The spiritual Side of Aso villa. The Spiritual Side of Aso Villa 14 October 2016. *The Guardian Newspaper.* https://guardian.ng/opinion/the-spiritual-side-of-aso-villa/

Billy Graham Quotes. (n.d.). BrainyQuote.com. https://www.brainyquote.com/quotes/billy_graham_161989

Bruce Lee Quotes. (n.d.). BrainyQuote.com. https://www.brainyquote.com/quotes/bruce_lee_378322

Council of Europe (2008). 12 Principles of Good Governance. https://www.coe.int/en/web/good-governance/12-principles

John C. Maxwell. (n.d.). AZQuotes.com. https://www.azquotes.com/quote/912350

Lee, K. Y (1965-2000). *From Third World To First: The Singapore Story 1965-2000.* New York: HarperCollins Publishers

Maxwell, J. C. (1999). *The 21 indispensable qualities of a leader: becoming the person others will want to follow.* Nashville, TN, Thomas Nelson

Ralph Waldo Emerson Quotes. (n.d.). BrainyQuote.com. https://www.brainyquote.com/quotes/ralph_waldo_emerson_12109

UNDP (1997). *Governance for Sustainable Human Development,* UNDP Policy Document, New York. https://digitallibrary.un.org/record/492551?ln=en&v=pdf

World Bank (1993). *Governance and development (English).* Washington, DC. World Bank Group. http://documents.worldbank.org/curated/en/604951468739447676/Governance-and-development